Apocalyptic Imaginary

The Best of Modern Mythology, 2011

Writing by:

James Curcio

P. Emerson Williams

Rowan Tepper

Mr. VI

Rusty Shackleford

Brian George

David Metcalfe

Wes Unruh

Cat Vincent

Gunther Sonenfeld

Doctor Adventure!

Conversations with:

Aunia Kahn

Charles Eisenstein

Raymond Salvadore Harmon

Layout, Design and Curation

James Curcio

Copy-editing

Michael Tesney

Photograph:

Rachel Reynolds

Special Thanks for donating $100 or more to

2011's Mythos Media Fundraiser:

Arild Stromsvag, Renee Beattie, Judith Curcio,

Nikolai Nothos, Fenwick Rysen, Joy and Benjamin Warren.

1st Edition published January 2012.

Mythos Media

www.mythosmedia.net

What is the Modern Mythology Project?

Modernmythology.net started out as my personal blog in 2005, though the ideas I've been exploring there have been gestating since early adolescence. It's become apparent to me in the years since that I'm not alone in many of them either, but that's getting way ahead of ourselves.

Over the years it has become an open nexus for discussion and analysis on the part of people who study and create modern myths. (We'll get to what we mean by "modern myth" later.)

Though several contributors have advanced degrees, we make no assumption that someone needs a Ph.D to be actively engaged in this work. In fact, many of the myths of 20th century academia— including the idea of a hard line between one discipline and the next— seem to pose a limitation that individuals need to overcome if they want to participate.

It is our hope that this project can continue to enter classrooms as well as people's homes, and that it will remain an open platform for the discussion and dissemination of original, forward-thinking work. Though a large extent of that responsibility falls on each of the contributors, it also falls on our audience, since this is not an entirely one-directional process.

The analysis we've done on Modern Mythology is the reflection of people who create media as a day or night job. Some produce video or music, write books, or even, much to Bill Hick's legendary disgust, work in advertising.

This was not a pre-packaged, planned strategy. Aside from some general direction, I gave each of the contributors the keys and told them to write what was meaningful for them. I herd cats, which as all cat owners will tell you, is a contradiction in terms.

Blog content is written with alacrity. It is written fast and furious with the hope that it isn't so riddled with errors that the audience feels like they're gazing dimly at the cypher stone of a forgotten civilization of drunkards. Sometimes you win, sometimes you lose. You just have to keep pounding, and keep the content running with enough regularity that people bother to check in on what head-candy you have for them today.

This book is an opportunity to give a selection of that material another polish, even if our DIY approach makes a stray typo here and there not entirely out of the question. Similarly, I have chosen to keep the style and format for each contributor as it was written, rather than fitting everything into the same mold.

A little more history. In 2006, P. Emerson Williams, Michael Szul, Tovarich Pizor and I joined forces to create Mythos Media, a platform for the production of modern myths that might slip through the cracks or be dismissed by mass-media publishers and outlets. Mythos Media was my third full-out attempt at helping to germinate an indie media collective. (Previous ones have led to shared A/V production facilities that are sadly no longer in existence, this one was more focused on virtual platforms due to the lower overhead.) Many years of hard work followed, where we produced and released books, comics, illustrated books, audio books with dedicated original soundtracks, albums, and collaborated a great deal with many other creative groups and production companies.

But there was an issue with our strategy. It became apparent that we were better positioned to help produce and incubate the *creative* elements of these projects than back them as a traditional publisher might. I guess I was looking to be a part of a movement, not a publisher and bean counter. And as artists ourselves, when our few investment options fell through, it became painfully clear that we simply didn't have the fiscal resources to do what we had initially set out to do.

That doesn't mean roll over and die. It means... try something different.

We made the concerted decision to maintain Mythos Media as a brand representing quality, off the path content. In February 2011, ModernMythology.net was opened up and made into a group endeavor, a site dedicated to maintaining a platform for the discussion of mythology and the independently produced media that follows from this discussion. Anyone involved can forge their relationships with whatever publishing or distribution approach best suits their project, as Mythos Media is no longer a publisher itself. This project began a creative collective, and it remains one, for all of those who are interested in joining and driven enough to play on the level.

Since February, the site quickly grew to a steady 20,000 - 30,000 visitors a month, all coming to investigate original content on mythology crossing and incorporating many supposedly disparate disciplines: art, writing, linguistics, philosophy, anthropology, systems theory, psychology, film. The sheer number of visitors doesn't represent a huge marketing success, as many world-class blogs such as The Huffington Post easily see more than that on even a slow news day . However, when you consider the subject matter and our approach, it seems to indicate an interest in a rather enigmatic subject.

Over the course of this project, and in the publication of *The Immanence of Myth* (Weaponized), we have been developing a curriculum for modern mythos which has even spread to the classroom at SUNY Binghamton and hopefully beyond. But what is the intention of this curriculum? What benefit can it serve?

The *Immanence of Myth* began this curriculum of self-discovery that reaches far outside the scope of academic inquiry, which *Apocalyptic Imaginary* continues. This is a challenge to us all to question our beliefs and dig into our own personal history to better understand our story, and our place in the modern myths unfolding around us every day.

This curriculum isn't a route to learning new facts. It's the first step on a path to transformational unlearning. Become who you are and live your myth.

The benefits of this sort of challenge will vary from person to person. Many will become infuriated at first, as they feel their beliefs challenged, and certainly many will react with a knee-jerk dismissal before they can ever get far enough in to realize what the potential benefit can be. This is not something that will get you rich quick, in fact the honest truth is that a deep rooted tendency to doubt and question everything will likely not make you very popular in the boardroom. However, that only further highlight how absolutely essential it is.

I have been told by many that this work has changed their lives. I hope that continues, and that this collection gets you thinking about old things in new ways. If so, I feel we've certainly done our job.

What you do with it is up to you.

James Curcio

www.jamescurcio.com

Myth in the Narrative

James Curcio

I've had many discussions with people over the past few years about why myth is important. Many of these come down to a misunderstanding about what the word "myth" means, so what could have been an interesting discussion about politics, permaculture, or even literature quickly deteriorates into a debate on semantics.

I'd like to avoid rehashing that argument, and toward that end, give a definition of myth that all of us can wrap our heads around. I hope as a result of it you will see why this is such a crucial issue to explore, as it has relevance in regard to all other disciplines of study.

First, I'd like to start us off with a short excerpt from the introduction of *The Immanence Of Myth* (Weaponized press). This excerpt was also published on the net in the art journal Escape Into Life as "Living Myths." I chose that title because most people think of myth as the study of classical myths, the study of what I would consider *dead* myths.

Modern myths are, quite plainly, *alive*. They represent not only our ideas about ourselves and the world around us, nor our beliefs of the same, but also and probably more distressingly, exist at that juncture that lies *between* these things, and which defy our plain view. Not quite pure fantasy, rarely easily understood as an objective or material force.

From that introduction:

> *We may use myths to explore why something is the way it is, or what we are to do with it, but a given myth remains just an interface. It is through us, through embodiment and direct interaction, that it is made immanent. There is no transcendent realm beyond the symbols, and in themselves, the symbols are empty shells. The myth is living because we are ever-changing and transitory. In other words, we are living, and myth too is living. It is a part of us, our mirror. It is like the moon in relation to the sun– without the sun, the moon would cast no light, but in the presence of the sun, it appears to have a light of its own. If this seems far-flung, consider this statement: coming world conflicts will be driven by ideological forces along cultural fault lines. In other words, by our ideas about ourselves, others, and the nature of the world we live in. Ideas are not just ideas, when they take hold of us.*

Framing myth in this light makes the discussion of the subject anything but "coffee shop talk." Modern myth is on the lips, minds, and knife-points of those in the midst of active revolution, as well as those working in media. In fact, all that is represented, all that we could form an opinion on as we form an opinion on it, is in that process entering the realm of myth. Doubly so when it is presented back into the world through discourse of any kind.

This is the perspective of myth from the cultural level.

You see, there are different scales on which myth can be approached.

I want to talk now about the less understood *personal* dimension of myth, since many of us are more familiar with how it seems to operate at the macro- level of culture. "Personal myth" is a term several of us started employing in the discussion of immanence and myth, which seemed natural but it has caused a great deal of confusion when it isn't clearly explained what we mean. It has come to have primacy in regard to myth through the lens of immanence rather than transcendence. Which sounds pretty erudite, I suppose, but it really isn't that difficult to grasp if we look at it headlong.

So what is personal myth?

Lately, I've taken to giving this example of personal myth when asked this question, because it is something so many of us have experienced it:

You meet someone and fall straight through the floor. You fall in love. Which means, you share a story with someone else. You are co-writers. Co-editors. And one of the preconditions of the plot is, "you're in love." That isn't to underrate the reality of that experience, at that time. Not at all. It is real. Real as any other emotions are real. Dangerous as any wild animal. But it is still a story, and our relation with one another depends a great deal on it.

You develop a shared myth about your lives together. Some of it is just in the expectation they'll be there tomorrow, or other day-to-day assumptions. Other myths might be about your shared future. You scope out houses, or fawn at the mysterious plants growing in someone's front yard. Anecdotes, shared memories remembered as-if you are the same being, dreams, trinkets representing your shared history ...

It may seem like your meeting could have been foretold in the stars because of its raw necessity. Falling in love is a deeply mythic process. Maybe that is why there are so many myths about it.

But sometimes, well, quite often, things go "wrong." Such as your partner doing something to lose your trust in them, however you define that. Let's say, for now that they run off and join the circus, or if you prefer the more likely scenario , let us say that they get wasted and bang some trash at a bar. Either way, your perfect story has just been re-written by some hack. Unfortunately that hack was your partner. Anyway...

For whatever the reason, the story twists.

Maybe the narrative is strong enough to stick to the story after the two of you fight for a while about plot structure. But if not, if the characters of our stories become too incompatible, now what? Now you have your arc, and they have theirs. Do they continue to work as a cohesive form, creating a specific story- No.

This is your *new* myth. To hell with the old book. Besides, some characters have to die, figuratively speaking.

Suddenly the whole relationship is a different story. Maybe they're even a villain now. It was a mistake, they are "a total asshole." And who knows, those assessments may be more accurate than the ones you made when under their spell. Now you have to call your friends and tell them the new story. Share it on Facebook. Re-enforce it in your music listening habits. THAT LYING SON OF A BITCH. Turn the music up.

Have you ever stopped and looked behind what you're doing? If so, I imagine you may have experienced something interesting. The force of these narratives is so strong that often you can be aware of the wizard behind the curtain, and *still* be subject to his capricious whims. For better or worse, we are trapped inside our stories, a hall of mirrors that only death frees us from. (Or not.)

But maybe you don't see behind these games we play with ourselves, and one another.

Either way, we go on thinking this posthumously written myth is the "true" myth. The most recent story is often the most appealing one. Maybe we're all just obsessed with "The New."

But all our myths are- at one time or another, in one way or another- equally true.

Take a breath. I want you to think about an ex-, and then recall yourself in the story you shared with them. Reify that story just for a moment, and pretend all your premises at that point in time were true. If you do it right, you'll either feel nauseous and dizzy, or like the linebacker from the Rams just sucker punched you in the kidney. You will likely find a wide range of myths that conflicted with one another when you were with them, and a different assortment of them.

Consider that these stories were equally true, equally untrue.

Hard to swallow, isn't it? We're all constantly changing our stories, and the fact that we pretend otherwise is one of the greatest scams about "human behavior" that popular culture seems to pull off. (And yet we have this delusion that we have somehow "evolved" beyond myth because of the centrality of science in how we think of the world around us.)

We re-write the past like this, and we do it so constantly that it is absolutely unimaginable that a sense of our history is anything other than a series of overlapping myths. Our experience is a palimpsest- that is it is scraped only partially clean and used again and again.

A palimpsest is a manuscript page from a scroll or book from which the text has been scraped off and which can be used again. The word "palimpsest" comes through Latin from Greek παλιν + ψαω = (palin "again" + psao "I scrape"), and meant "scraped (clean and used) again."

There are many more esoteric ways of explaining what a myth is but this is the most direct. It's a part of the process by which we come to know *anything*, because we have to make assumptions and make a story of things to understand them and understand our place in them.

Consider this except from a New Scientist article:

"We are our narratives" has become a popular slogan. "We" refers to our selves, in the full-blooded person-constituting sense. "Narratives" refers to the stories we tell about our selves and our exploits in settings as trivial as cocktail parties and as serious as intimate discussions with loved ones. We express some in speech. Others we tell silently to ourselves, in that constant little inner voice. The full collection of one's internal and external narratives generates the self we are intimately acquainted with. Our narrative selves continually unfold.

State-of-the-art neuro-imaging and cognitive neuropsychology both uphold the idea that we create our "selves" through narrative. Based on a half-century's research on "split-brain" patients, neuroscientist Michael Gazzaniga argues that the human brain's left hemisphere is specialized for intelligent behavior and hypothesis formation. It also possesses the unique capacity to interpret– that is, narrate– behaviors and emotional states initiated by either hemisphere. Not surprisingly, the left hemisphere is also the language hemisphere, with specialized cortical regions for producing, interpreting and understanding speech. It is also the hemisphere that produces narratives.

Narratives are, once they've become embedded or repeated, no different from myths. There may be some sense in considering myth to be a narrative that has been repeated, and solidified with belief. If you find yourself confused by our use of the words "myth" or "mythic," try the word narrative instead. There are slightly different connotations. Myth means "by mouth," it is that which is spread. A narrative feels somehow less grandiose. But those connotations are aesthetic– rather than intrinsic.

So, understanding that personal, national, cultural, spiritual myths all operate similarly at different scales, at least structurally, we can see that mythology is not a topic relegated to one discipline, but is instead an open discussion that could benefit as much from exploration of cognitive psychology as from the analysis of literary symbol or the direct experience of a shamanic ritual.

In all cases, the operative word is *literary*. The Modern Mythology project seems to be based on this single premise: that we can gain a more complete picture of the human puzzle by looking at life as we look at fictional stories. This is not science, nor is it meant to replace science. It is instead meant to shed light on the range of epistemological, ontological, and psychological realities that quite simply cannot be parsed by the scientific method. That doesn't make these realities less legitimate. Phenomena require no proof on their own ground– after all, analytic logic rests upon tautology– but when we seek verification, repetition or explanation, then myth comes into play, whether or not the model it presents creates a satisfactory representation of that phenomenon or not. This draws a line between the method of science and most everything else, which we discussed in *The Immanence of Myth* and look at again with new eyes.

The principal idea at work here is an imagined contention between science and the humanities, and that one is more valid than the other. As I expressed in what I hope was a more lucid way in "Is Myth Dead?", this contention is a specious one, although the distinction is not. The success of the world-views supported by scientific discovery have been so complete that the common understanding of "science" has invalidated all that is seen to be outside the scope of scientific scrutiny. Again, the core of modern myth is the absence of myth. A purely scientific attempt at experiencing or interpreting literature would be as pointless as using Lord Byron to get us to the moon, if maybe not quite as dangerous. (Don't let him put the bear on board.)

Modern mythology is not a strictly philosophical project. However, we see philosophy itself as a form of "meta-literature," which replaces personal narrative with generalized abstraction. We build this assumption upon the points explored in *The Immanence of Myth*, though for our purposes here we may be able to borrow from Mauthner's philosophy as paraphrased in *Wittgenstein's Vienna*,

> The idea that there exists such a thing as logic, in the sense of something universal and immanent in all languages, is another illegitimate reification. Belief in such a thing, even though it appears to comprise a body of knowledge, is superstition. "Everything about thinking is psychological," Mauthner insists; "only the pattern [Schema] of our thinking is logical." However, the pattern of man's thinking– and of his speaking, which is the same thing– is determined by, and reciprocally determines, the culture in which he lives, as both develop simultaneously; it is not something pre-existing which can be derived from "immutable laws of thought."
> **Wittgenstein's Vienna, Janik and Toulmin.**

This is a big idea, and deserves adequate consideration. Despite appearances, there is a point in this endeavor beyond philosophy or sophistry, but the point may not itself be what it seems. Regardless, this makes the project of philosophy and modern mythology virtually indistinguishable except for in this regard, where the former uses rigor and the latter additionally embraces the truth of the single instance, the irreducible, the ephemeral, rather than that which has been generalized by a rational process.

There is a natural desire to draw strict boundaries between "narrative," "myth," as well as the mythologization process itself, and philosophy. However, we have worked hard to avoid that desire, instead drawing the contours out slowly and through extensive demonstration that you can find in *The Immanence of Myth* and this work.

The distinction between personal myth and all other forms of myth remains a misleading one.

> *Precisely because the cosmos can be understood and interpreted only through the human spirit (ed: so far as we are concerned) hence through subjectivity, what would seem to be the purely subjective content of mythology has at the same time a cosmic significance.* **Cassirer, Philosophy of Symbolic Forms Vol 2.**

This is drawn from Schelling's observations about myth. Indeed, some academics might recognize in our work on immanent mythology a philosophical underpinning that seems derived from applying so-called postmodern critique to Schelling's idealism. This is not inaccurate, though I think it pigeonholes the scope of this project more than I would like. That philosophical position has only arrived through years of working directly with these ideas in practice, (producing and reflecting on the production of media), rather than by prescriptive design.

> *[Myth] is objective insofar as it is recognized as one of the determining factors by which consciousness frees itself from passive captivity in sensory impressions and creates a world of its own in accordance with spiritual [or psychological] principle. If we formulate the question in this sense, the "unreality" of the mythic world can no longer be said to argue against its significance and truth. The mythical world is and remains a world of mere representations–but in its content, its mere material, the world of knowledge is nothing else. We arrive at the scientific concept of nature not by apprehending its absolute archetype, the transcendent object behind our representations, but by discovering in them and through them the rule determining their order and sequence. The representation gains objective character for us when we divest it of its accidents and demonstrate in it a universal, objectively necessary law. Likewise, in connection with myth, we can only raise the question of objectivity in the sense of inquiring whether it discloses an immanent rule, a characteristic "necessity."* **Cassirer, Philosophy of Symbolic Forms vol 2.**

This sums up the essential position of immanent myth from which we can move forward without further concern about "objective truth."

I hope this re-appraisal of myth leads us to new ideas and questions which none of us would have formulated on our own. It is a group endeavor and benefits the most from the interaction of minds in the commons.

What it is, what it becomes, is as much up to you as it is to me.

James Curcio is a transmedia freak of nature coming to a screen near you.

He has produced a diverse range of projects including collaborative novels and graphic novels with associated immersive media/marketing campaigns, albums, unorthodox podcast and audiobook series, web magazines and group blogs, and interactive CDs. Much of this work is distinguished by its signature aesthetic and irreverent style, and has been published by a number of independent presses.

www.jamescurcio.com

An Apocalyptic Vision

James Curcio

When I was sixteen, I started writing what became my first novel, *Join My Cult!* (New Falcon Press). I didn't realize at the time, but it was my first attempt at rendering some of my personal mythology:

> *...Yet I was finding, to my amazement, that I was not alone in these woods, or in my need to find a myth with real, personal value. Alone all of my life, estranged from any sense of greater community, I was overjoyed by this. But I really had no idea how to proceed with it, or how to broadcast this message to all of these wanderers, winding their own paths to a center, an end which is still unknown to us all. What we are looking at here is an apocalypse. Spiritual, cultural apocalypse is much more subtle than mushroom clouds, fallout, and radiation burns. People can deny it. No statistics can prove it. The only evidence we have is a feeling of profound loss, and hope for a future that does not reduce the qualitative values of life to quantities and for companions to share these stories with so that they can have value, and pass on to our children in the next world. Reflecting back on this, I believe many in my generation have been so called . Not because we merely want to be important, but because we know that we are coming down to the wire.*

If there is one thread that seems to tie together the articles we've written over the past year, it is the theme of apocalypse as personal revelation. This is not merely a collection of pessimistic fear-mongering. Looking back now, I can see this theme clearly, passing from one mouth to the next. In different ways, we all voice the necessity of cooperation and community on a personal and very real level, juxtaposed against the backdrop of a dehumanizing corporate and consumer culture. Much of this book is an attempt to examine the imaginary dimensions revealed through apocalypse, thus the title.

We speak of apocalypse rather commonly these days, it seems to be a part of the zeitgeist of this age. Yet many seem to have only a cursory or rather simplistic idea of what the reality– and the concepts we use to encapsulate that reality– entail. Let me help clarify.

The destructive force the precedes apocalypse does one of two things: the rupture either creates an ouroborous, so that the currents of the past can re-shunt into the future, or it provides a true break in which an entirely new process can begin. A galaxy can whirl about itself in seeming harmony for billions of years, and then "collide" with another in such a way that the stars therein don't collide, but the two galaxies mutually annihilate, sending some stars whirling off into the void while others remain to start a new show. This is in our own distant future, as Andromeda and the Milky Way approach their death-dance.

The emphasis on destruction seems to be distracting to most people. It's the same with Shiva– how easily people forget the "all be-getter" part when they hear "all destroyer." They lose the actual sense of the symbol, much as "myth" becomes simply "an untrue idea," "apocalypse" becomes merely "the end of everything." Not so!

The apocalypse is not in the explosion, the rupture, it is not the initial catastrophe but rather what exists in the silence afterwards. Apocalypse is that revelation. Another example might be seen in the times during our lives when we think things are a certain way, and we operate under the mandates of that myth, until suddenly we are shown in a stark and often painful way that those illusions will no longer suffice. However, if you can brave the passage with your eyes open, for even a split second, you will be offered the opportunity to see the truth without its clothing, before we again begin wrapping it in myth, a new myth.

Another example comes to mind, which incidentally and eerily fits the Tarot imagery of the Blasted Tower. After the World Trade center was blasted to the ground, many in the States, certainly many in New York, witnessed something interesting. In the weeks that followed, we looked at one another with new eyes. We were snapped awake, startled as if out of a dream, and though frightening, there was also a sense of possibility, even hope, in those new eyes, and in seeing our old neighbors in new ways. Of course, the predominant culture over the years that were to follow fell into a myth of fear and hate, and that rhetoric shrouded over any real apocalypse that could have been. At such times we are forced to transform, but the actual nature of that transformation is not certain.

In a purely spiritual sense, this is why towers are shattered. I'd like to leave you with a short passage from *Join My Cult!* Which, it's worth noting, was written *before* 9/11:

White walls are here because they caught me Working.

Bombed the Hive building.

The flames danced and sang about me.

Something the Agent said came back to me then, a commentary, a running monologue: "Millions of souls were freed from slavery to the Great Eye, Novus Ordo Seclorum, Eye of Shiva, blaster of towers... Of course the gate-keepers brand me a 'terrorist.' It is no matter. Through the power of association the entire structure will topple in due time. This is high ritual, and the ultimate sacrifice for the survival and evolution of my species, which I love so dearly. Even my friends and teachers have disowned me. Horus, the bull of your father is avenged. We can now return to our mother, whole. The dove resides within the blasted tower, and within that destruction, that madness, we lay the seed of the purest aspect of life..."

The whole structure erupted in a final, defiant exhalation, breathing out foul, billowing columns of smoke. Its systems coughed and spluttered. The whole world was dancing and singing. We sang:

Alas! With ruthless hand you have destroyed this fair edifice... it falls and decays!

And then, right before the cops came, we started a chant. It just came up out of nowhere...

In the temple of the temple of the temple of the Holy
sits a woman who is waiting who is waiting for the sun
in the temple of the temple in the temple of the
Holy creeping shadows falling darkness she is waiting for the sun.

For the people of the people by the people making people
in the temple of the temple of the temple of the Holy
She is weeping for the people of the people
making people in the temple of the temple in the temple of the sun

The possibility of Apocalypse also presents itself in our perception of time. While, from a scientific standpoint, time is a sort of grid within which events occur at discrete intervals – x1, x2, x3, ...– without qualitative distinction, from an apocalyptic and mythic standpoint, time is measured by the ruptures that identify different eras.

So, from the Christian standpoint, we live in a time defined chronologically from the chaotic moment of Christ's birth until the point of his return. (Interesting that it should be from his purported birth and not death, since much of their symbolism is based around his crucifixion.)

It may be easier to grasp this concept if we view it from the perspective of our personal life, as we identify "eras" by the institutions that rule our lives for periods of time (such as during high school or military service), or when we are in a relationship with one person, and then others. The very characteristic of our experience during one period may be qualitatively different than the next, so that we might ask "who was I?" when we look back upon a past "era" from the privileged perspective of the present.

This would seem to highlight an event that characterizes those points in time— but in an apocalyptic sense, they are characterized most of all by that point when a previous historical framework was destroyed to produce the new one— every invocation is a banishment, and each step toward one thing is a step away from something else.

Myth, Undead:

The Apocalyptic Imaginary

Rowan Tepper

The apocalypse is sublime. This is no great leap of thought, for not long after he wrote the *Critique of Judgment*, from which I derive my understanding of the term "sublime," Kant wrote an essay entitled "The End of All Things." A direct translation of the Greek ἀποκάλυψις as "lifting the veil," or as "revelation" suggests that the concept of the sublime may help shed light upon the persistence of this eschatological myth in secular, (post-) modern culture. Apocalypse was always something more than a theological concept– the object of our fascination, anticipation and even desire has only taken new forms throughout history: the Bomb, unprecedented epidemics, "the end of history," the ultimate fate of the universe, the end of the Mayan calendar... even the zombie apocalypse. The idea of apocalypse is strangely *attractive*– sublime, surpassing nature.

Compared to any of these scenarios our ability to resist becomes an insignificant trifle. Yet the sight of them becomes all the more attractive the more fearful it is, provided we are in a safe place. And we like to call these objects sublime because they raise the soul's fortitude above its usual mediocrity, and allow us to discover within ourselves an ability to *resist* which is of a quite different kind, and which gives us the courage to believe that we could be a match for [their] seeming omnipotence. [2]

The apocalypse is immanent– as a more-or-less thinly disguised myth. The apocalypse is always imminent– as an event ever on the horizon. Always yet to come, this imminence signifies our safety– it is a formal structure of eschatological myth: nothing that happens can be the apocalypse, rather the apocalypse is fundamentally what does not happen– immanence itself revealed, unveiled and disclosed. [3] In what time I have today, I shall speak of apocalyptic myth as not only "our symbolic interface with the world, often but not always presented in allegorical or metaphorical form," [4] but as a narrative form that functions, as it were, as the plot (μῦθος) of history. The apocalypse would be the climax, *dénouement* and closure of a particular history: judgment, revelation and end.

The zombie apocalypse is trendy– Facebook tells us that 599,332 people have RSVP-ed. [5] It is the latest form of the apocalypse– a postmodern incarnation of the myth with modern zombies. While folkloric zombies have a long history and various cultural forms, "modern zombies are often related to an apocalypse, where civilization could collapse due to a plague of the undead" (Munz, Hudea, Imad & Smith, *When Zombies Attack!*). [6] This was an entirely new vision of the end when *Night of the Living Dead* appeared in 1968, the year during which post-industrial, post-modern capitalism attained undisputed ascendancy after the failed revolts of May.

The zombie apocalypse is the eschatological event most fitting to post-modernity – being tongue-in-cheek and altogether lacking in seriousness, we can laugh off the very real anxieties it nevertheless signifies. While it is doubtless true that the sources of this anxiety– our mortality and the very real capacity of our civilization to annihilate itself (attained with the advent of the Bomb, object of other forms of the eschatological myth, enduring element of the contemporary apocalyptic imaginary)– are inextricably bound up in every such myth, others appear to be more significant.

Modern zombies are American– the largely interchangeable zombie flick settings signify an automated, atomized and alienated society. Modern zombies embody the undead afterlife of modernity and its myths– the alienated subject, no longer properly an "individual," lives and labors like an automaton. The ideologies of post-modern liberal capitalism produce and rely upon subjects such as these– zombies with a pulse.

The modern zombie is the apotheosis of the Cartesian subject in a world in which the Enlightenment project and modernity have revealed themselves in the end to be bankrupt. Atomization and alienation are not merely the result of ideological operations– for, with the flight of the divine of which Hölderlin was prophet and Nietzsche apostle, the subject can no longer have any certainty concerning the world and others. The (post-) modern subject has never since free of false consciousness.

The zombie apocalypse is an allegory of the final triumph of the ideologies of post-modern capitalism. What leaves us in fear and trembling is the possibility of becoming a working zombie with a pulse in a monkey suit. The apocalyptic sublime serves both as a call to arms– *vive la Résistance*– and as a promised, imminent return of mythic lost immanence.

Killing zombies is just plain fun, too.

The zombie apocalypse heralds not just the end, but the annihilation of history. The mutism of the (post) modern zombie signifies the irrevocable loss of language– that fickle mistress that first led human civilization from primordial Chaos to the Cosmos of myth, then from exile to the millinery Kingdom of Judeo-Christian theology, and thence into our times. Of course, the sum total of this inheritance has since passed into and come to give shape to the practices of both history and politics: eschatology– secularized– takes the form of the ideology of progress that has long deluded "the left." In Germany, during the 1920s and 30s the SPD remained convinced until the bitter end that Hitler and the Nazis represented a temporary aberration and that the country would "come to its senses."

While Neoconservatism has fallen out of favor and is scarcely taken seriously outside of a few remaining enclaves, its theoretical underpinnings and fundamental myths have not. The political philosophy and philosophy of history to which Neoconservative thinkers and politicians have subscribed are in truth a particularly theatrical and shamelessly bare-assed instance of the dark inverse of the ideology of Progress, by means of which many cling to the wreckage of Modernity and the Enlightenment project.

While for the progressive, justice, utopia, apocalypse, etc, etc, are thought to be part of an inevitable future End of History– a Last Judgment that will brook no more delays, the Neoconservative, begins with and builds upon the extremely idiosyncratic reading of Hegel's Phenomenology of Spirit developed by Alexandre Kojève in his 1933-39 lecture course at the Sorbonne, later published as "Introduction to the Reading of Hegel," in 1947, as transmitted through Leo Strauss, Francis Fukuyama, etc. According to this line of reasoning, the vanguard of humanity has, in fact, already reached the end of History, and all that remains to be done as a political task is to bring the rest of the world "up to speed" (c.f. Iraq, Afghanistan, etc. That all went according to plan, right?)

Here, Kojève's words are every bit as intelligible as my own:

> *The disappearance of Man at the end of History... is not a cosmic catastrophe: the natural World remains what it has been from all Eternity... nor is it a biological catastrophe : Man remains alive as animal in harmony with Nature or given Being......the end of human Time or History– means quite simply the cessation of Action... the disappearance of wars and bloody revolutions. And also the disappearance of Philosophy; for since Man himself no longer changes essentially, there is no longer any reason to change the (true) principles which are the basis of his understanding of the World and of himself. But all the rest will be preserved indefinitely; art, love, play, etc, etc; in short, everything that makes Man happy.*

A. Kojève– footnote to the first edition of **Introduction to the Reading of Hegel.**

Post-historical humanity would thus be "happy zombies," as it were. For, with the cessation of Action, the disappearance of Philosophy and the end of Becoming, language would become superfluous, mere glossolalia.

According to a footnote added to the second edition, which happened to appear during that fateful year that saw both Kojève's death and the release of *Night of the Living Dead*, this apocalypse signifies the post-historical epoch during which the Lion of American Capitalism shall lie down with the Lamb of Soviet Marxism (or vice-versa): One can even say that the United States has already attained the final state of Marxist "communism," seeing that, practically all the members of a "classless society" can from now on appropriate for themselves everything that seems good to them, without working any more than their heart dictates.

I was lead to conclude that the "American way of life" was the type of life specific to the post-historical period, the actual presence of the United States in the World prefiguring the "eternal present" future of all of humanity. Thus, Man's return to animality appeared no longer as a possibility that was yet to come, but as a certainty that was already present.

[1] Immanuel Kant, "The End of All Things (1794)," in *Perpetual Peace and Other Essays*, Trans. Ted Humphrey (Indianapolis: Hackett, 1983), pp. 93-106.

[2] Immanuel Kant, *Critique of Judgment*, Trans. Werner S. Pluhar (Indianapolis: Hackett, 1987), pg. 120.

[3] Georges Bataille, "Beyond Seriousness," in *The Unfinished System of Nonknowledge*, Trans. Michelle Kendall & Stuart Kendall (Minneapolis: University of Minnesota Press, 2001), pp. 212-218.

[4] James Curcio, "The Immanence of Myth– an Anthology," *Escape Into Life*, January 27th 2011.

[5] As of January 31st, 2011, around noon.

[6] When Zombies Attack!: Mathematical Modelling of an Outbreak of Zombie Infection", by Philip Munz, Ioan Hudea, Joe Imad and Robert J, Smith?. In *Infectious Disease Modelling Research Progress*, eds. J.M. Tchuenche and C. Chiyaka, Nova Science Publishers, Inc. pp. 133-150, 2009.

Rowan G. Tepper is Adjunct Lecturer in the Department of Comparative Literature at Binghamton University. He is the author of the essay "After God: The Revolutionary Absolute," in The Immanence of Myth, and previously of Michel Foucault: Toward a Philosophy and Politics of the Event (2010). Somehow they let this loon teach. He considers it his job to corrupt the youth of various parts of New York State.

Modernism to **Postmodernism** to

Postmortemism

P. Emerson Williams

"Lady Gaga killed sex," says the once much-discussed Camille Paglia. She quotes her subject who declaims "Music is a lie," "Art is a lie," "Gaga is a lie." The death of the novel is an idea so oft repeated that one can envision members of the literary establishment daring each other to intone the phrase three times in front of a mirror in expectation of the Candyman to appear. We cultural types do love to declare death wherever we cast our jaded, blood-shot eyes. When our imaginations are exhausted, hard-ons for the latest arising require new extremes of fetishism.

And closer to home for us, the right honourable psychonaut James L. Kent says "we've come to rest after years of the deceler8ing [sic] of music as a living mode of expression." [1] Nice opening shot.

Every style of traditional, ethnic, and world music has been incorporated into the modern pop uber-genre, a black hole from which little seems to escape. There are no more Afro beats, throat singers, Middle Eastern microtonal scales, Buddhist Ohms, Irish sea shanties, American folk songs, or Navajo ancestral chants that haven't already been chewed up, digested, and shat out by modern pop composers.

Forcing sound snippets into a twelve-tone, four on the floor format is for sure a denigration of these traditions, but it's a very colonial Western POV that would consider that this raiding of sampled sounds a canceling out of entire traditions of music and culture.

I recall a thread in an occult social site that began from a post that stated that Eastern philosophies were being killed by Western adoption through Western seekers not understanding the finer points or getting entire belief systems wrong. Well, I have news– taking a photo of a person does not trap their soul in the camera and Americans weaving Tibetan Buddhism into candy-coated self-help material doesn't make all the monks in exile disappear from the Universe.

Maybe he's right. Perhaps the hum that is plaguing many towns across the globe with no detectable source is just the musicological equivalent of the smell of dead plague victims piling up.

Arthur Krystal is a voice in the "Death of the Novel" chorus for some time. In an interview in Harper's magazine he expands his theme:

> *Leaving film aside, since it's a relatively recent art, the arts as we know them have run their course. You can argue this until your face is blue, but it won't change the historical fact. Time and technology wait for no artist, and unfortunately history has seen fit to alter our sense of time by the invention of new technologies.*

Philip Roth has devoted his life to creating novels, but he's pessimistic about their future.

"The book can't compete with the screen," Roth tells Tina Brown in this video, and even the Kindle won't change that.

"It couldn't compete beginning with the movie screen," Roth says. "It couldn't compete with the television screen, and it can't compete with the computer screen."

Krystal does admit that this could be in part a personal issue, though. In what appears on the surface to be the similar line of argument, Nick Currie wrote in his blog a few years back that the realm of popular music is an endless exercise in what he termed retro-necro. All a re-hash of old ideas, established forms entirely lacking in innovation.

Said Mr. Momus:

> *There's a very simple, very big problem for today's pop musician: if you fail to attack the father and rip up his rules, the father will always beat you. He will beat you because he did what you're doing first, with more spontaneity and passion, and with less reverence. If you fail to rip up the rules of your father's pop music and start again, you will see pop music becoming what classical and to some extent jazz have become: interpretive art-forms dominated by performers who simply run through a canon of set masterpieces.*

The retro-necro argument is very different, though. While claiming development and innovation has not been occurring within popular music, he is writing from a point of view that this is not only needed, but also very much possible. Altermodern means Western art will be rescued by assimilating the work of artists outside the Western canon. As if Cubists and earlier movements were not doing this generations ago. The answer to retro-necro is to throw out that canon entirely. Forget the necrophilic worship of mouldering rock stars and discard arts previous incarnations.

Postmodernism's endless production of hybrid beasts was an admission of defeat in the face of not knowing where to explore next. So, are we post-cultural, post-production, post-industrial, post-historic, post-consumer, post-toasties...? The *feuilleton* age has come to a conclusion and music is verily the final cultural corpse to be assimilated by the Glass Bead Game.

Looking at who is digging into this scorched ground, it seems that what we have here is 40 to 60 somethings telling the kids that they can go home because we did it already. We're tired and the most compelling myth to the most intellectually exhausted among us is that we built it, we trashed it and the rubble is not worth bothering with.

It occurred to me when soldiers and tanks were sent into Tiannanmen Square that this was done partly because the old men in charge didn't want what they had given their lives to to disappear with their last breaths. It may be natural to want one's age to be the concluding chapter and the rest of time to be the happily ever after. If it is true that the first generation to never die is in the wings, as has been said, these immortals could turn out to be the biggest pains in the ass for those joining them later. Just as the rich want to keep it all. That's why they bought our governments, after all. Have we reached our full capacity for creation and development? Is there nothing ahead but technocracy and narrower permutations of master-slave relationships until the final death-rattle?

We're stuck in a loop of end-time pornography and can't see beyond it, but anything not only can happen, but it *must* happen. This static death-march can only come to a conclusion and what's on the other end of it are events that can only arise there. Survivors will do things that were never done before. If humans are not around for much longer, we can be sure the last moments of the last human will be experienced with a head full of brand new stories.

[1] Writing for Acceler8or, the new transhumanist vehicle established by R. U. Sirius.

P. Emerson Williams is a writer for Dominion magazine, the host of the Necrofuturist Transmission on Nightbreed Radio, editor and producer for Music Tuesdays on Alterati.com, core member, sound design, actor, artist and composer with FoolishPeople and is currently working with FoolishPeople on the feature film Strange Factories. Williams is product development manager and art director for Weaponized , the publishing imprint of FoolishPeople. He is also a visual artist whose work has graced book covers for Original Falcon, Weaponized and Westgate Press, the pages of magazines including Culture Asylum, Isten 'zine, Ghastly, Esoterra and too many more to list, album and CD covers for Rat King, a Primordial/Katatonia split 10" EP on Misanthropy Records, SLEEPCHAMBER and his own bands Veil of Thorns, Choronzon and kkoagulaa. He has worked with Manes and John Zewizz and is currently recording two albums with SLEEPCHAMBER.

Red Riding Hood

Neurology, Narrative & Storytelling

Mr. VI

Once upon a time, half-way back and a little off to one side; this is where the stories live. Are you sitting comfortably? Then I'll begin:

Stories are a form of communication, and they open doors. Doors to understandings and concepts that are unbound in time– their relevancy shifts according to circumstances, environment and culture.

> *To understand and remember stories, readers integrate their knowledge of the world with information in the text. Here we present functional neuroimaging evidence that neural systems track changes in the situation described by a story. Different brain regions track different aspects of a story, such as a character's physical location or current goals. Some of these regions mirror those involved when people perform, imagine, or observe similar real-world activities. These results support the view that readers understand a story by simulating the events in the story world and updating their simulation when features of that world change.* **Psychological Science August 1, 2009 vol. 20 no. 8 989-999**

Read that again:

Some of these regions mirror those involved when people perform, imagine, or observe similar *real-world* activities.

Certain parts of your brain do not discern between "reality" and "fiction." They simply create and act. Further:

Verbal communication is a joint activity; however, speech production and comprehension have primarily been analyzed as independent processes within the boundaries of individual brains. Here, we applied FMRI to record brain activity from both speakers and listeners during natural verbal communication. We used the speaker's spatiotemporal brain activity to model listeners' brain activity and found that the speaker's activity is spatially and temporally coupled with the listener's activity. This coupling vanishes when participants fail to communicate. Moreover, though on average the listener's brain activity mirrors the speaker's activity with a delay, we also find areas that exhibit predictive anticipatory responses. We connected the extent of neural coupling to a quantitative measure of story comprehension and find that the greater the anticipatory speaker–listener coupling, the greater the understanding. We argue that the observed alignment of production- and comprehension-based processes serves as a mechanism by which brains convey information. **PNAS August 10, 2010 vol. 107 no. 32 14425-14430**

Before there was written text or visual media such as film, stories were the primary method of cultural transmission:

"The speaker's activity is spatially and temporally coupled with the listener's activity."

Let these two statements combine in your head for a moment; see what they point to– scientific speculation that a story can draw you in, change your perception and have an effect on you.

Suddenly the idea of the magic word doesn't seem too far fetched, does it? Immerse your listeners in a narrative and it becomes their reality. Expose them to it every day to reinforce it– this is the province of politicians and news anchors the world over.

If you go deep enough, the statement "it's not real" loses potency. Of course it does, because your brain is modeling it "as if", and some stories are extraordinarily old.

From a 2009 article in Britain's *Daily Telegraph*:

A study by anthropologists has explored the origins of folk tales and traced the relationship between variants of the stories recounted by cultures around the world.

The researchers adopted techniques used by biologists to create the taxonomic tree of life, which shows how every species comes from a common ancestor.

Dr Jamie Tehrani, a cultural anthropologist at Durham University, studied 35 versions of Little Red Riding Hood from around the world.

Whilst the European version tells the story of a little girl who is tricked by a wolf masquerading as her grandmother, in the Chinese version a tiger replaces the wolf.

[...]

Contrary to the view that the tale originated in France shortly before Charles Perrault produced the first written version in the 17th century, Dr Tehrani found that the variants shared a common ancestor dating back more than 2,600 years.

[...]

The original ancestor is thought to be similar to another tale, The Wolf and the Kids, in which a wolf pretends to be a nanny goat to gain entry to a house full of young goats.

Let's think about that:

Red Riding Hood is a modern iteration of a story that's older than the Christian religion. Its themes and characters have inhabited the human consciousness for longer than the dominant religious narrative on this planet of approximately 7.2 billion human beings.

Here at Modern Mythology, we've talked much about werewolves, witches, zombie apocalypses and vampires lately. We've given nods to *Twilight*, to *Buffy:The Vampire Slayer*, *True Blood* and more; pop-culture narratives, flirtations with the shadowy Other– these are wildly successful in capturing money and attention.

Millions of people the world over have synchronized their brains in similar ways as they've been drawn into the narratives, and so I find myself wondering– is this actually modern at all? If our brains become spatially and temporally coupled with the tales, are we in fact moving in myth-time, sacred *kairotic* time?

If stories can be modeled on taxonomic lines, then familial structures apply– then each generation partakes of some of the others.

This year, we see a new iteration of *Red Riding Hood*– a film released in March, directed by Catherine Hardwicke, of *Twilight* movie fame no less. As the second trailer for the new Red Riding Hood film states in blood red letters: HOW CAN YOU KEEP OUT WHAT IS ALREADY IN?

Gary Oldman's werewolf hunter Father Solomon makes much of what we've discussed about the terror of the monster explicit in the trailer:

"The real killer lives here, in this village– it could be your neighbor."

And even this current version owes much to an earlier predecessor– its structure and plot appears to be strongly influenced by the 1984 film *The Company of Wolves*.

"The worst kind of wolves are hairy on the inside and when they bite you, they drag you with them to hell."

Contagion and the *Outsider on the Inside*– the deepest fear of any community. Is it any wonder that deception is often classed as morally reprehensible? Consider then what seemingly innocuous actions might somehow become imbued with a sense of the sinister if a strange affect occurs.

Imagine what would happen if that which forms groups– the act of communication, of coming together at a fundamental, even neural level– can be used to alter and manipulate individuals and the group itself?

Might this skill be viewed with suspicion– the very act of alternative narrative-construction becoming potentially morally dubious, and even synonymous with evil and falsehood? Even the notion of "a fabrication" seems to imply something less than righteous; an *ersatz* version of events which gives the concept of myth its general pejorative sense, doesn't it?

And thus myth and myth-makers are at worst reviled as liars, frauds and mountebanks, and at best regarded as irrelevant and perhaps semi-entertaining because of their ability to make people feel emotion. Even spin-doctors and political speech-writers are somewhat scorned by the general populace, and they and their siblings in the advertising industry are either ignored or derided as manipulative individuals whose sole goal is money– something which alienates them from the general populace.

Which means, as aliens, they often are perceived as faintly sinister– they operate in the murkier realms of the human psyche, away from the clear and rational. In a sense they are lunar and mercurial– both in the planetary correspondence sense, and the adjectival. They take the enlightened solar construction of language, born of the neo-cortex, and use it to produce movements in the deep emotive dark of the reptile brain.

What's more, they do this in such a way as to hijack the investment in the rational, non-mythic narratives– the same machinery that models "reality" can be used to create and work with the mythic precisely because, as already noted, parts of the brain cannot tell the difference!

Due to this this investment in the rational narrative, so-called irrational or mythic narratives must be treated as second-class in modern society, because to do otherwise is to suggest that the dominant narrative may also be a made thing– a fabrication in the truest sense of the word.

This would, apparently, undermine an awful lot of important things.

Imagine, if only for a moment, what would happen if all narratives were created equal. Imagine if Merlin stood shoulder to shoulder with Einstein, or Zeus went for a stroll with Michael Faraday and they met Thor and Benjamin Franklin chatting about super-heated plasma?

Those who prefer a singular narrative might say that such a moment would be a retrograde step, a movement back to the dark ages of superstition. Yet that moment exists every time we spin a tale and immerse ourselves within it– the data seems to confirm what we already know!

We speak spells, we weave worlds from songs and stories. If it's any kind of movement, it's not merely retrograde because it goes so far back as to be beyond any world we can conceive. It's so far back it's looped around and met the deep future, and the only way we can get to that space is to perform an act of willful imagination.

Beyond superstition lies hyperstition; fictions that make themselves real in the place where the eldest ancestor meets the last child of mankind. Both are creatures so far beyond us that they are literally dreams, which means that every time you step into that dream-time, you are with them as part of a community which is hard-wired into the very heart of our brains. (So to speak.)

If that isn't a damn good pedigree for a myth-maker– to be standing amongst wizards, sorcerers, shamans , storytellers and poets from the Before and After It All– then I don't know what is.

So think on that, as you browse this book, as you cruise the corpus of the contributors here, and maybe muse on it at the cinema or the next time you become engrossed in a story regardless of media.

Then feel yourself carried away by the spell, or admire the lay of the charm with a professional eye.

Because it doesn't matter which you do when it happens; every time you are drawn in, you're only being human, and that's a very interesting thing to be– however you look at it.

I'll leave you with a quote from the introductory voice-over to the wonderfully odd 1974 film *Zardoz*:

> *In this tale, I am a fake god by occupation– and a magician, by inclination. Merlin is my hero! I am the puppet master. I manipulate many of the characters and events you will see. But I am invented, too, for your entertainment– and amusement. And you, poor creatures, who conjured you out of the clay? Is God in show business, too?*

Be seeing you.

Mr VI is a writer and philosopher living in the North West of the UK. He enjoys employing furious schizotactical analysis in almost everything, has a beard, and (usually) wears a broad-brimmed hat. He has written essays and poems for various publishers, including The Immanence of Myth (Weaponized) and his current book, due out mid 2012. He blogs periodically at www.cold-albion.net and is fairly sure bits of his brain are clinically dead.

Vivisecting Verses

DARPA Investigates the Neurobiology of Narratives

David Metcalfe

If I were a betting man or woman, I would say that certain types of stories might be addictive and, neurobiologically speaking, not that different from taking a tiny hit of cocaine.

William Casebeer of the US Defense Advanced Research Projects Agency (DARPA) in Arlington, Virginia

Despite the fact that it's readily apparent Mr. Casebeer has never tried cocaine, DARPA's current interest in narratives is an interesting development at an agency known for unique scientific inquiries. On April 25 and 26th DARPA held a conference called Narrative Networks (N2): The Neurobiology of Narratives. The purpose of this conference was to follow up a February 26th event which sought to outline a quantitative methodology for measuring the effect of storytelling on human action.

We owe much of the early development of the internet to DARPA, along with remote viewing, remote controlled moths, invisibility cloaks and other wonders of the contemporary age. Now they've got their sights set on stories, and we can be assured that, in the near future, there will be some fatly funded scientific justification for what we already know.

That's the unfortunate thing about these scientific inquiries, they're often years (usually centuries) behind the times. I seem to recall an author who spent his entire career developing this theory, and effectively influencing television, film and music with his ideas. Who was that? Something about word viruses? Oh, yes, William S. Burroughs. Who in turn got much of his inspiration from other thinkers like Brion Gysin, Alfred Korzybski, and really beyond all this name dropping, what true poet or writer doesn't understand the fact that their writing takes on an effective reality?

The Medieval Italian philosopher Giordano Bruno wrote a treatise, called *De vinculis in genere* (Of Bonds In General), which has been used at the London School of Economics. It may be written in Latin, but it details these exact theories and, if our scientists today were properly literate, everything there is perfectly quantitative. They don't even have to be bilingual. Cambridge offers a perfectly viable translation that I'm sure would be easily accessible via any local library.

In fact, Bruno's theories are merely the quantification of the European bardic arts, Grecian theatre, and Egyptian ritual, which were themselves already quantified, encultured forms of earlier story telling techniques (and that's just within the Western tradition).

So what's new here? What secrets of the narrative art will be unveiled in this quantitative analysis?

Nothing much, other than what was once an art-form will suffer yet another reduction into a somewhat less effective means for moving markets, and manipulating populations. It is that reduction, in the end, which is really the goal. For all the money they spent on remote viewing tests, Russel Targ, one of the lead scientists during the SRI tests, admits that it's fairly easy to do, and that the most telling instruction manual they still have on the subject is a centuries old yogic training manual from India.

I ran across information on this symposium from a link posted by Joseph Matheny (who has himself demonstrated the ability of storytelling to motivate action) to a brief article on Dollars and Dragons. The piece contains links leading on to other posts, one on Verilliance, a blog about "Better Marketing Through Science," and one from a professor of Narrative Philosophy who has been studying this phenomenon for 30 years.

While Casebeer states the purpose of the project is to develop an understanding of how narratives effect the development of terrorism and violent behavior, with the attendant goal of creating *"counter-narrative strategies."* If his understanding of a little nip of yao is any sign of his social savvy, it's obvious that there are others with less noble goals who will gladly leap on these developments and ride them for all they're worth.

Rest assured, however, these quantified tales will stink from being stripped of their true marrow. It's doubtful DARPA will be able to add anything new with an MRI or EKG strapped to the head of some already desensitized citizen, or college kid looking for a couple of extra dollars to pay rent. Hustlers have been doing that every day on the streets to grab a few bucks for a beer, or a hit of heroin, and poets and proselytizers have been banking on the same principle for over a millennium.

What we need today is the actual passion of the storyteller, which is the direct encounter with the mystery of storytelling that will be missing from any state funded exploration of narrative theory. I was surprised to read the positive reaction of the narrative philosopher to these DARPA inquiries, and the use of neurobiology, to explore this realm.

DARPA is late to the game already, with marketing firms and corporations having spent millions on testing the neurobiological importance of just about everything we encounter during the day. The inherent ethical violations in this would seem to spark the heart of anyone who'd read more than a smattering of philosophy, and I'd hope in 30 years the engagement was somewhat deeper than a facile overview.

This kind of naiveté is what has provided the gate for so many horrible violations in the past, and continues to be a pressing issue. The narrative philosopher comments in her post, "*for someone like me who has researched and written about Narrative Philosophy (philosophy involving the phenomenon of storytelling) for close to 30 years, with special emphasis on Narrative Ethics, it is particularly gratifying to watch the latest developments in neuroscientific research concerning the human urge to tell stories.*" Really? That's incredibly silly of you.

But that's just it. There's no room for reality in the mediated realm of inquiry formed by government and universities. It really is up to us, as individuals, to tackle these issues within our own lives. Seeing something like this come up is merely a call to action to apply what we already know. You can wait for the official response or get out on your own and explore these ideas within the rich history that's already afforded to them.

Whatever you do, know that there are powerful influences out there (with a lot of money behind them) that are looking into how and why you appreciate a simple story.

David Metcalfe is an independent researcher and artist focusing on the interstices of art, culture, and consciousness. He is author of *"Of Dice and Divinity– Some Thoughts on Gambling and the Western Tradition,"* an essay in *The Immanence of Myth.* Writing and scrawling regularly for The Eyeless Owl, his illustrations were brought to life in the animated collaborative grotesquery A Serious Enquiry Into the Vulgar Notion of Nation featured at select venues in downtown Chicago during the Spring and Fall of 2010. He contributes to Evolutionary Landscapes, Alarm Magazine, Reality Sandwich, The Revealer, and is currently co-hosting The Art of Transformations study group with support from the International Alchemy Guild.

The Myth of the Artist as a Young Man

James Curcio

In the *Immanence of Myth*, I wrote a great deal about the impact that the symbolic characters of Dionysus and Lilith have had on my life. I felt that this would be the most accessible way to bridge the gap between old and new concepts of what mythology is. We also spoke about our personal mythologies, as some of us have in this project as well, over the past few months.

However, I didn't provide any personal myths which have no specific literary or historic origin.

So, I'm going to share a bit of my personal history with you, awkward as it may be to open up to an unseen and unknown audience. Or maybe it's easier this way. After all, the confessional has an intentional element of anonymity to it.

Normally, this kind of perspective tends to have more meaning to the author than it could for someone else. That is the reason I chose to keep it out of that book. But I will share these things with you, the nameless, faceless public, if for no other reason than it helps to demonstrate what I mean when I talk about living mythology, or how deeply it permeates our lives, our motivations, our histories, even our bodies. In other words, I'd much rather this make you wonder about *your* own story or myths, rather than fixate on mine.

But we only know the world through the interface of our own personal myths, when it comes down to it. I'm just saying, I don't need you to stare at my reflection for me to believe I exist.

So, here's a salient personal narrative: the origin of the myth of myself as an artist.

I was born the only child to a single mother. My father was excised, you might say, at the age of four. Despite his statements to the contrary– occasional phone calls from out of nowhere, promises that never manifested into anything tangible– he never reappeared in my life, and died in 2007 of leukemia. His life and death left little impression on me except the sadness of losing something you never had. I'm not sure if there's a word for that in English, but it's an unusual feeling.

I have always had a proclivity for creativity. You might call it a fixation. I've always had a sophist streak, and I've always resolutely done my own thing. My mother has plenty of photographs of me as a young child drawing, typing at a typewriter, practicing my moody artist stare, slumping under a gravestone with a devil's mask on. (Alright. She set that last one up, but I believe the others were spontaneous.)

I can look back and say I was always an artist. But certainly I didn't think of it that way. How can someone be driven to do something so socially detrimental and personally reckless as proclaim they're an artist or writer and, heaven help them, try to make a living doing something like that? It's ludicrous.

I'd like to find some of the roots of that belief, and like most roots, it meanders. Many of them are long. Come along, if you like.

My mother was a photographer and artist. I have many memories of growing up with nude models or photographs around the house, and from that I got a strong association between eroticism and creativity, rather than eroticism and guilt, as so many other people seem to have. I don't mean the photographs were lewd, though there's a sexualization process that occurs whenever a photograph involves nudity. My point is, she wasn't a pornographer. (Or at least not in my presence). But I never saw anything shameful or dirty about nudity or basic sexuality. I didn't realize what a gift this was until I was older.

Exposure to the non-sexualized female form had a generally positive effect on my orientation, especially in regard to women. I've had the hunch that many men develop misogynistic tendencies due to the social forces that pull them to be a part of the "men's society," as such there is separation anxiety from the mother and the male must distance himself from all signs of what are perceived as femininity. At one and the same time, many heterosexual men are terrified by the power women have over them. There are many examples I could provide to support this claim, but let's just say that it's something I've also observed within our own society, and I decided to stay on the "Mommy" side of the fence.

Which is not to say I didn't psychologically separate from my Mother– though I did so probably later than many– but rather that I decided never to associate myself with anything simply in terms of it being perceived as masculine or feminine. If I want to wear pink I'll wear pink. If I want to strap bull horns to my head and wrestle greasy, sweaty men...

Well. I can happily say that's not something I want. But by God, if I *did*...

Even the rhythms and schedules of my body seem to be geared towards fugues and periods of intense creativity, when they are listened to, and physical and mental instability and misery when they're not. I've always been nocturnal, or at least given to bursts of energy late in the night. This, too, has always been the case, and nothing short of strong drugs can change it for any period of time.

As a child this meant stealing sharpies and drawing pictures all over the walls of dinosaurs doing battle with one another, or grabbing twine and stringing up all my stuffed animals– I had a whole menagerie and naturally they all had personalities and back stories– and pretending I was a spider from Mirkwood.

My Mother's girlfriend at the time, if I remember, got furious, and chased me around the house because I refused to take a pillowcase off my head. I can't remember exactly what the thought was, but I think I may have been a knight.

That's just how kids play. I'm not saying there's anything unusual about how I played. But so many have it beaten out of them, others grow out of it. I didn't do either. (Though I'm not wearing the pillowcase right now, because I can't wear it and type at the same time. Plus, people get the wrong idea when bald white guys start putting pillowcases on their heads.)

The point is, in fundamental ways, who I am hasn't really changed. It never has nor can I imagine that it ever will.

But how that nature has been interpreted as I've aged has changed. As I've grown older this has become more of a problem in a society focused entirely on widgets and dollars. As I entered adolescence, this was of real concern to my mother and her girlfriends, who realized, as I began to, that there may not be a ready-made place for me in society once I left the nest. This concern was prescient but futile. At the age of 32, I'd say that if nothing else I am fully committed to my narrative, no matter where it may lead. It is simply too late to try to start at the beginning and re-write the script. I've got it right here and nowhere in it does it say "entertainment lawyer" or "database programmer." I'm as trapped within my myth as anyone else.

When a person is a certain way, certainly if they're like me, the more you try to push them to be unlike themselves, the more firmly they take hold. As I grew older, male peers tried to enculturate me– play these games, don't play these, wear these colors, not those– and I resisted. When they tried to enforce their rules with violence, I rebelled first simply by ignoring them, and finally by caving in to their methods and defending my right to play with whom I wanted, how I wanted, with violence myself. They left me alone.

I had a real fixation on science as a child, and devoured information like food and drink. When I was into dinosaurs, I learned everything I could. When it was sharks, I learned all their Latin names and wanted to know which sharks evolved from what predecessors. Their fierceness was part of what attracts young boys to such things, but I also remember feeling a kind of reverence for their beautiful, single purpose. All predators share this trait, a fearsomeness, the desire to embody it, is part of that attraction. Sharks never cease moving, prowling, hunting, devouring.

I suppose this was around second and third grade. Teachers thought I had a learning disability. I couldn't read at all, until my mom started reading me *The Lord of the Rings* and I discovered something that captured my imagination. I jumped to a college reading level seemingly overnight. Again, this is a personality trait that hasn't changed since day one. If I'm not engaged, not a single word gets in, no matter how much it might make my life easier, or how much I might wish it were otherwise in the circumstances. Engagement doesn't always mean pleasure. But without it, it's like there's a wall between myself and whatever it is I'm supposed to be doing.

I imagine it is this way for many of us, and our education system is simply woefully inadequate. Children shouldn't have to be tricked to learn. They are *engineered* to learn. Of course, the nature of what they're primed to learn is very different at different ages. At any stage, not boring the living crap out of them is a good place to start.

My mother, as I said, was an artist. But she made great sacrifices to keep me alive. She did whatever had to be done, including taking house painting and tedious drafting jobs in locations where the fumes gave her incredible headaches and, for all we know, central nervous problems. As the years passed she had to give up more of her creative pursuits for the sake of our mutual survival. She once told me that I was the primary reason she stayed alive. I'm not sure how some people would react to that but for me it struck me, as the years have passed, simply with a deep desire to make my life count for something. It has to be something beyond toil, eating, shitting and dying like the sharks, or else what was that sacrifice for? Like most everyone else, I have taken jobs to keep the lights on, but when they suck the light out of my eyes and make the real purpose of my life impossible, I have to move on.

At first, I didn't plan on being an artist. The myth began, rather, that I would be a great scientist. I had an excellent science teacher in 6th grade that got me into astrophysics, and physics in general. I loaned college physics books out of the library, figured out what I could with tutors– like a friend's father who worked for NASA– and got interested in fission and fusion reactions. I wanted to help design a generational starcraft. (Of course, I was really into *Star Trek: The Next Generation* at the time. And even back then, I'm pretty sure I thought Wesley was a dork, Data wasn't fooling anyone with his "I can't feel emotions" thing, and it was a little... *queer* that Picard kept a real riding saddle in his quarters "just in case.")

Then, another fork in the road. I took a test which in our public school determined the future course of our academic careers. I placed high enough to be on the honors science and math track, but the teacher and I didn't get along, and she put me in the lowest rung instead due to "emotional troubles." I lost any and all interest in science and became absorbed by fantasy and art once again.

As I grew older, I found myself falling in with the typical outsider groups that form in high school. My attention was equally divided between girls, fantasy novels, guitar, roleplaying, and philosophy and occult books. Dorktopia.

All of this was leading towards a certain crisis point.

Throughout my childhood I had a close relationship with my Grandfather. Or so I thought. I was his only male heir, and to him, that was a big deal. He was a high ranking Mason, and had become wealthy by his own hand. (Life insurance. His first company went bankrupt but the second took.) He once owned a farm, which is to say a large plot of land, with Arabian horses. I got to ride them though it was my cousins and aunt who became the equestrians.

That's not really relevant. More to the point, which will become clear eventually, my Mother and Grandfather always had a very tense relationship. He had been abusive – emotionally and, in the distant past, physically. Money still remained a method of control, as it often is between those who have it, and those who don't. When she didn't do what he wanted her to, she would be penalized. By proxy, so would I, though I didn't understand at the time. Money is also used as the great legitimizer. If something can be monetized, it has value. If it can't, it cannot possibly be of value. This cultural myth has remained the single greatest bane of my existence from birth until the present moment.

Eventually, a subtle tug-of-war that I was only vaguely aware of as a child between my Mom and her Dad was threatening to put us out of a home. We moved to the country with my Mom's girlfriend at that time. It may not have been a log cabin but in some ways it wasn't as far off as you'd think. Our source of heat was a wood stove. Eventually we graduated to coal.

Don't worry. I'm going somewhere with this.

A day came, after my sixteenth birthday, that I visited my grandfather. He sat me down and told me that it was time. Time for what? I wondered. He launched into a speech about the time for boys to become men. And he asked me what I was going to do with my life. (As if a sixteen year old would normally know such a thing.)

As it so happened, I *did* know. I proudly proclaimed– "I'm an artist." At a given time, I explained, maybe I'll be doing music, or writing, or visual art, or all of them. Maybe working on films in some capacity. But at bottom I'm an artist. That's where my passions are, and it's the only way I know to be and find meaning in my life.

His face turned red. He screamed at me for an hour, telling me I would "shovel shit all my life." It's still unclear exactly what he meant by that, but he repeated it enough that I remember it to this day, still recalled with that initial, visceral sensation of confusion. Some of the other words he used I did understand. That I was a loser, a failure, and that I would always be a failure.

He disowned me that night, and I never saw him again, until the day of his death, when I looked on his urn but still only had the chance to recall him from photographs. I tried to remember the countless summers I had spent in his presence. He taught me to fish, to shoot. I'm sure he would've taught me to drink, if given the chance– he was a real champion at that– he also taught me to golf, although I'm not quite sure how golfing is more valuable than painting. But all I could think of was that night he told me that I would never succeed at anything, that I may as well kill myself then and there and spare us all the trouble.

He used those words.

Much of my extended family is dead now but those who survive try to minimize it, saying that he just lost his temper, maybe he didn't mean it. But I know that of all the things he said to me growing up, he meant nothing more than the words he spoke to me that night.

I attributed the brief hospitalization in 1995 that got me started on *Join My Cult!* to a bad reaction to Prozac and a breakup, but I can also paint a straight line from those words to the crisis that put me in there. I could draw a line, even, from that moment to the present.

There is no way he could understand my psychology so well as to have done it intentionally, but with those words my Grandfather ensured I would become the embodiment of what he was most terrified of my becoming. I guess if any of you have gotten some use out of my creative work, you can thank him... though of course he just set the hook.

However, this did not make me an enemy of sound business sense. I made many attempts to learn and succeed in the world of business, and in the process I have learned a lot about advertising and marketing, about pricing strategies, about competition and cooperation, about management. But at the bottom of it all it's been something like infiltrating enemy headquarters and learning their methods. From that day forward, though I had been primed for it since my birth, my goal has been to prove him wrong.

So, sometimes when people ask me what I do, I say I am keeping the family business alive. They smile and nod, or ask "what business is that?" They probably assume I mean a rat compacting factory or something. When they ask me that I give them something particularly confounding to chew on a while, generally some gibberish invented on the spot. Teleportation. We've been working on teleportation for generations. The truth is just that it's a long story. Did you make it to the end? Do I need to draw a line between the stars, and paint a constellation? Our myths determine our motivation, our purpose, our meaning.

Grandpa liked to drink. So to that end, I say "Cheers, Bob." I'm having a glass in your honor at this moment. You helped make me the incorrigible bastard that I am today. I very well otherwise could have been stuck doing something tedious, like working as an engineer. Maybe I'll die in a gutter yet, but at the best of times so far, it's been goddamn weird. And I hope it gets a lot weirder before the end.

But this isn't just about me. I'd like you to think about the stories that tell how you got to who you are today. Don't assume these stories are true, of course; what truth they contain is a mix of your internal narrative and history. But the deeper we drill down into these myths, the more we distance from the layers of persona painted atop the mantle. What underlies the surface, our ego, we will talk about more later. For now, there is still exploration to be done in unearthing the structure of personal and cultural myth.

Confession of a Fugitive

James Curcio

I've been big on confessions lately. There's much we can learn from one another by being honest, even if we give ourselves a certain poetic license with the form that honesty takes. So bear with me a moment.

I've already revealed how I came to identify as an artist. I first started thinking about this because I asked UK-based artist Laurie Lipton a similar question in an interview for *The Immanence of Myth*, "Was there a sudden point when you realized 'I'm an artist,' or has that always been with you?," and it occurred to me that I had never asked *myself* that question.

Being an artist seems like no big thing, but it takes a real psychological shock to stick with it.

> *Being an artist doesn't take much, just everything you got. Which means, of course, that as the process is giving you life, it is also bringing you closer to death. But it's no big deal. They are one and the same and cannot be avoided or denied. So when I totally embrace this process, this life/death, and abandon myself to it, I transcend all this meaningless gibberish and hang out with the gods. It seems to me that that is worth the price of admission.* **Hubert Selby, Jr.**

That sentiment rings true for me. At the same time, you don't get on a path that requires such a commitment without having a psychological reason for following it. We have to be tricked or cajoled by fate. For him, it was ostensibly being laid up in a sanitarium for four years with tuberculosis. For me, an alcoholic Grandfather. Either analysis is actually specious. Our latent traits are like fuel for the fire of our lives. Countless little events conspire to create the narrative. In retrospect we may pick one or two and choose that. You see, though what I wrote in the previous chapter is true, it is just one myth. I could take many other single events in my life and use them as an explanation with equal validity, making quite contradictory claims. This is one of the elements of personal mythology that must be understood. They are, like stories, both true and false.

Do we really want to atomize and dissect ourselves into a series of anecdotes born from our personal history?

I certainly don't.

"A" (for artist) isn't the only scarlet letter I've sewn to my chest. Though I admit it selectively in public, close friends and lovers know that I also identify with another unfavorable term: philosopher.

If you didn't shudder or laugh at that proclamation, I imagine you don't have a pulse. I can't blame you, but let me at least try to explain myself before you get out the pitchforks or tell me to cut my hair and get a real job. (I went bald at twenty-four, so genes beat us all to it.)

I want to talk openly about ideas, and about writing. I don't know any way to do that but to confess my sin openly rather than have it leak out a little at a time. Clearly the importance of this issue goes far beyond me. I'm just starting from within the personal sphere because it is the one we know best, when we're being honest.

Being a philosopher is an orientation. We hope such signifiers give a liminal glimpse at that most mysterious companion in life, ourselves. Whether or not that is the case, I know it comes off as pretentious to proclaim "I'm a philosopher." Maybe it's a little like pretending you're a wizard or a silver dragon. Worse, a philosopher might be someone that is trying to put themselves on par with a bunch of illustrious, stuck up dead men. Not all of us can be Socrates, and if we have any sense of self-preservation, it's probably for the better.

> *Indeed, the crowd has for a long time misjudged and mistaken the philosopher, whether for a scientific man and ideal scholar or for a religiously elevated, desensualized, desecularized enthusiast and sot of God. And if a man is praised today for living "wisely" or "as a philosopher," it hardly means more than "prudently and apart." Wisdom– seems to the rabble a kind or escape, a means and trick for getting well out of a wicked game. But the genuine philosopher– as it seems to us, my friends?– lives "unphilosophically" and "unwisely," above all imprudently, and feels the burden and the duty of a hundred attempts and temptations of life– he risks himself constantly, he plays the wicked game–*
> **Frederich Nietzsche**

If we slander philosophy, maybe it shows a bias that has burrowed so deep into our culture that it's gnawed right down to its brain-stem.

I imagine cultural bias is the real root of the anxiety that "philosophy" evokes. There's no good reason why anyone would want to identify with such a thing in America in 2011. We have learned to only value what leads to the illusion of quick and easy profits, even if most of us are quickly going broke chasing that illusion with staggering debt and empty dreams.

I'll take a shot at explaining this cultural obsession, but I think it is such a vast topic that it could easily be the subject of a book. So, instead, I'll pull a quote from an episode of *The West Wing* as I am prone to, without warning or clear cause, from time to time:

> *Toby: You're a good father, you don't have to act like it. You're the President, you don't have to act like it. You're a good man, you don't have to act like it. You're not just folks, you're not plain-spoken... Do not– do not– do not act like it!*

> *President Bartlet: I don't want to be killed.*

Toby: Then make this election about smart, and not... Make it about engaged, and not. Qualified, and not. Make it about a heavyweight. You're a heavyweight. And you've been holding me up for too many rounds.

The point is: it is not accepted in American popular culture to be an intellectual, let alone a philosopher.

So, let's be clear. I'm proposing no universal qualification for this label. Maybe some of this objection that says "plain spoken" is somehow more "real" is justified. I don't mean that an intellectual need be a member of the intelligentsia. I don't mean we need obscure degrees or bullshit postures of righteousness because you are the leading Sanskrit scholar. The virtue of philosophy isn't dependent on holding a popularly arcane belief, degree, or qualification.

Those are some of the true pretensions of academia. A philosopher is simply engaged with ideas. We should all be philosophers, in addition to whatever else we are – lovers of wisdom and skepticism, passionately exploring ourselves, willing to knock one idea against another until we come upon something interesting, or our eyes start to bleed and our hands turn to dust.

It is a sickness of the academy to use philosophical debate as a thin veil on top of the primate territorial bullshit that drives *Hoi Polloi*. I've often felt like the social dynamics seen in chimp groups is not at all unlike the posturing of inter-departmental groups in academia. There's something refreshing about the directness of an ape that smashes his rival over the head with a firm length of wood. Professors do the same thing with the minutiae that lesser mortals couldn't possibly comprehend. "You're not a *real* scholar," these people might say, "you don't even know Latin."

No, I do not. But I have the curiosity required to hear "Hoi Polloi" used in conversation, and not knowing what it meant, I looked it up. After a while it became part of my conversational vocabulary. None of us should be afraid of admitting what we don't know.

We should be terrified of not having the balls to admit we don't know it, realize it isn't a pissing contest, and look into it. In reading De Landa's *1000 Years of Nonlinear History*, I encountered a vast number of systems theory terms I was unfamiliar with. I highlighted each one and did some casual research. In the process, my underlying perspective of the world shifted. It's as if I looked up from the pages of the book and found myself in a world of complex and irregular systems all interacting with each other in a world of infinitely reducible scale. I hope that some of you will do the same as you work your way through this book, if some of the material in the following pages is unfamiliar to you.

Let's not be afraid to raise our hand, to not know, or to be flat out wrong. Let's instead uphold the dictum "Question Everything" and admonish the tendency toward mental laziness.

When in doubt, we should not level blank *ad hominem* attack, but rather turn an idea around on its head and try it another way. A myth of cooperation that fosters dialog, rather than one of competition, fostering habitual unthinking? That isn't widely accepted in our society, at least from what I can tell, and that's a horrifying thing. Too many of us spend far too many hours regurgitating at one another, but no one is listening.

I want to make dialog an intrinsic part of *our* myth.

"Stupid" we can all fix simply by accepting the staggering weight of our epistemological uncertainty, the gravity of what we don't and simply cannot know. We're all a bit stupid one way or another. (I was outsmarted by a two year old the other night.) Apathetically ignorant, on the other hand... nothing can be done about that.

Nothing can be done about a posture of superior cynicism either, embodied best by the legions of semi-illiterate culture police that wander the hallways of the Internet waving a big old bat of stupid at anyone with the audacity to produce creative work they don't care for. These people want to knock everyone else down a peg, rather than work together to lift ourselves up. Nurturing conflict has always been the forge of creative communities.

I remember having my nose squashed on my face like a cherry tomato for reading too much when I was a child. I'm stubborn. It only made me want to read more. Some things never change, but I'll never understand why being mentally engaged is received with such hostility, why the lowest common denominator is God of the modern proscenium.

Or maybe I do know, and I simply don't want to accept it. We are easy to manipulate through common and base needs, and few of those have anything to do with knowledge. The truth is often depressing, and the core myths of America is only sustained at this point by the delusions of endless profit and unlimited resources. It is a fictional Happiness machine. Whatever "America" once meant, philosophy is clearly anti-American today.

Aside from being a decent way to pass the time as we chug coffee, the value of philosophy resides in the questions we learn to ask. We learn to disassemble any and every idea that comes our way, we learn to build castles of thought that can withstand just about any siege, and at the same time realize how *arbitrary* it all is. You can hang Foucault's Pendulum anywhere. Our ideas and beliefs arise through an ongoing relation with our environment, which includes each other. (Emotions are another monster entirely, although there are some interesting links between emotions and beliefs. Subject for a later piece.)

So, it's easy to conclude that all philosophy is just 'armchair pontification.' After all, many of us can and do spend a vast majority of our lives fighting over mental and linguistic territory that has little actual bearing on *life*.

Let's formulate this anti-intellectual sentiment and look for some kernel of sense. It's easy to say "get real." More commonly people say, "drop the semantics." Even some philosophers have taken this tack, defining from the outside in rather than the other way around, relegating truth to a game of language which is either well formed or incoherent within the context of that game.

Okay, I'll bite. There are many dangers hidden within the escape into metaphysics, as Mach claimed, "any duality is a sign of the metaphysical, any absolute is a conceptual phantom." But what's *real* here?

For instance, is this idea that the *real* is what we taste, touch, and feel just a form of new Empiricism? Or when our parents said "the real world," they actually meant *money*. If either of these is correct, what makes it any different than the empiricism that lived and died under 18th and 19th century British Imperialism, or systems of logic and economics that say that all that does not fit the system is irrelevant? Is "reality" something we can "get" at all, and how do we validate these claims as opposed to others? What framework do we employ when we–... And we're off to the races. Get your Pall Malls, espresso and weird looking French men ready.

I've been through this process myself and I think it's a little comical. You haven't sidestepped philosophy by proposing that We Act Now. (Supplies are limited.) Even the inquiry into the purpose of philosophy is an act of philosophizing.

But let me give you a hint: If you *don't* reflect upon your motives, thoughts, emotions, or the reality of your experience in any way, you're the behaviorist machine that corporations (and especially advertising execs) have dreamed of. Just shovel in those myths, boys. These freaks will eat anything!

That's right. The method of philosophy will never lead you to singular truth but it might keep you from being the foolish patsy of megalomaniacal madmen. Dismiss it at your own risk. If you want to spout rhetoric about freedom, learn to think for yourself.

All actions have positive and negative outcomes, different in type and scale from individual to individual. Handing out pamphlets, blowing up a building, or masturbating for the next twenty years all may be "right actions" according to the myths that infect your biomass. What's *your* yard stick? Who is to say unless we bring it into a context and hash it out? Does it change when contexts change, as they often do, from minute to minute? Does it change when our emotions shift, or when our orientation towards a belief changes?

Again, this is the *value of debate*, a truly lost art, which has been reduced in the political sphere to sound bites and emotional triggers. Debate is not *personal attack*, or empty intellectualism, a bunch of critics sitting around showing the world how clever they are by pissing on anything within range. It is an ongoing *relation* that requires equal parts defense and reflection, honesty and posturing, changing frames from specific contexts to the general and back again, considering outcomes, and the ways that groups of unique individuals with totally different ideologies can come together for a common goal, and accomplish it without ultimately caving in, giving in to one fascist will, and thereby either losing those unique qualities of the individuals involved, or splintering into warring factions before something valuable has been produced. (Splintering, dissolution, or what is known as negrido in alchemy are all important parts of the process. Nothing lasts forever.) Endlessly *questioning everything* is what keeps us fresh, even if we change our mind tomorrow when a better argument is provided, or when the scotch isn't readily available.

This process also happens to be iterative, if we do it right, so we're not going around and around like the moon. No, we're more like a bunch of drunken sailors, meandering through time.

There's no stopping point, and no identifying armbands. I've yet to meet a friend I completely agree with if we are willing to drill down deeply enough into our beliefs and ideas. This is because the collection of elements that formed us are all different. The debates we have, without ever presupposing that any one of us can ever be right, are one of the most crucial ways that we learn from one another. My best friends have challenged me, and they've done it with the greatest respect. As Robert Anton Wilson said, "Communication can only happen between equals."

We don't run from reality when we question it. We enliven it, engage with it, so long as our hearts and minds are in the right place. And what's the "right place"? ...

You see how this process never ends, and though many professional philosophers (academics) may find what I'm saying in this article distasteful, as it–to a certain extent–demystifies an Ivory Tower position, and in that ungrounding could be seen as inciting the plebes to think they too could explore such a privileged endeavor. Quite to the contrary of the ideal of Plato's Philosopher King, I say that philosophy is for everyone. The real junkies can call themselves philosophers, but all philosophers are to one extent or another "playing-at" philosopher, which is well and good so long as they don't think it lifts them to the heavens on dove's wings.

Reflecting on life is, quite plainly, the only philosophy that has any meaning after Wittgenstein so boldly declared he'd killed Western philosophy in one stroke. He used logic to demonstrate the limits of logic, and as a result, many have drawn the conclusion, as I have, that logic is not after all the central tool of the philosopher interested in existential questions.

This is an oversimplification. Let me explain. Though its proper interpretation is still much refuted, it still is a matter of historical fact that in 1922 Ludwig Wittgenstein wrote the *Tractatus*. Though it is far from the only symptom (or cause? who can get that straight?) of the growing schizophrenia produced by various ways of "knowing" the world, it is an easy place to start. It was, in retrospect, the beginning of a *kairotic* event. Which is somewhat ironic, considering that it is an almost unreadable book.

In other words, in logic-language it delineated that which falls under the project of philosophy, and that which doesn't.

Or does it? Wittgenstein himself seemed to quickly recognize the problem with his formulation, as we see expressed in *Wittgenstein's Vienna*,

> *The logical positivists (ed: analytical philosophers) were overlooking the very problems about language which the Tractatus had been meant to reveal; and they were turning an argument designed to circumvent all philosophical doctrines into a source of new doctrines, meanwhile leaving the original difficulties unresolved.*

Also of relevance to the point is this quote from the following paragraph from *The Immanence of Myth*,

> *While the positivists took Wittgenstein's early work as a call to expand only upon the principles of what can be philosophically expressed by logic-language, there is ample evidence that this is precisely the opposite of his intentions, as in many ways that which falls into the realm of myth, or what he called the metaphysical, was the real task of philosophy. In this light, perhaps the Tractatus was initially proclaimed by its author as the final work of philosophy not because it heralded the success of philosophy, but rather because it announced its boundaries, which as a whole hearkens its general failure!*

> *The realm "of which we cannot speak clearly" contains, among other things, the very mysteries of existence and consciousness which are to a certain extent forever unknowable no matter what models science invents to explain its machinations. The goal of myth is to point towards this mystery, without having any particular goal to unclothe it. Rather, it seeks to garb it in new ways. This is the realm that myth is best suited to. However, there is no parallel to be found within the positivist view; a view which we can, in the context of culture, relate to both science and industry. This can be seen in the positivists interpreted of the Tractactus,*

For the pragmatical-minded men of 1920, on the other hand, the absolute moral individualism which represented the unspoken point of the Tractatus was, quite simply, useless. For their purpose, all that appeared important in the book was the parts that could be put to constructive use ... The sweeping away of the old Central European dynasties had left a new world waiting to be built– on the scientific and cultural, as much as on the political plane. Positivism, one might say, is the utilitarianism of the philosophical rationalist– the metaphysical, or dogmatically antimetaphysical, justification of an empirical pragmatism that other men "accept upon instinct."

Reflecting on life is not just the task of the philosopher. It is also the task of the writer. So, abstract ideas and personal history both are the stuff of literature.

When we talk about ideas, we are really talking about ourselves.

Literary authors and philosophers are both fugitives of pop culture.

Variations on a Theme

James Curcio

Moving forward, I'd like to look at once at the concept of theme against the backdrop of the failed Enlightenment Project. Consider this a catalyzing thought experiment to get you looking for themes in your personal mythology and the cultural myths you've been steeped in. So to begin, tell me if this is a normal conversation to have while standing with the other groomsmen at a wedding,

"Never before has there been a generation of Americans so disillusioned by the American Dream." This was a friend of mine, out of work well over two years.

"Maybe in the 20s? It's hard to compare." By this point I too had surpassed my 99 weeks.

"Totally broken down. You can see it on everyone's face. We all know we've been had."

I was fidgeting with my sleeves. I'd never worn a tux before. "Just going through the motions. So. What you been doing lately?"

"Mixing cement."

I'm not sure this was a normal conversation, but who wants to have those? Beautiful wedding, otherwise, at least what I remember through the haze of pain medication. But he had a point, didn't he? Arguably that dream was always a bill of goods leveraged by the blood and sweat of the poor, but never before has the general public so generally recognized that *we've been had*. Many feel the downward slope yawning before us, as peak petroleum, an Empire over-extended, and an unstable climate push us into a troubled and horribly wondrous near future. Or so it might appear. Our future runs through our past, and we may reflect on the past so as to conjecture about the future. In the first century AD, there were revolutions within Rome that made its history seem bleak. I imagine in times like those, it seems like the entire world is about to end. As it turned out, those were the explosions that birth a sun, not its death throes in nova. That wouldn't come for three or four centuries, when the Visigoths helped dismantle an already collapsing empire. It should come as no great revelation that systemic change comes about...systemically. Call it the hand of God, if you want. There will always be "the Visigoths," in one form or another. Just as it seems there will always be fascists, the great organizing principle of Empire. Are we now standing at a transitory point, bridging the gap to a new beginning, or is this the final breath before the plunge?

We don't truly have the clarity of hindsight that might come from living a couple centuries, so we can never know what our future holds. Writers are lucky in this regard. What we don't know, we can invent, and feel no shame for the imposition of personal experience against the flimsy bulwark of statistics as sole arbiter of history.

We can ask: what light could history shine on this *feeling* of an Enlightenment lost, perhaps before ever reaching any real apex?

A question like this can very easily lead you to a novel, if you let it. Theme is ephemeral. We can only dance around it, like thirsty hummingbirds.

There's truth to how we answer existential questions, at least to the extent that all myths are true on their own grounds. Always. To the extent that you believe in them, at least until that moment that reality yanks us off our feet with a hefty tug on that bit in our mouths.

That is the kind of question that fiction can let us explore freely, posing endless what-ifs, myths that begin with elements of personal or world history, but that spin off in whatever direction we'd like. So far we've only been looking at this macroscopically. I think we all know what this feeling of "Enlightenment lost" feels like on a personal level– we reach for something, nearly grasp it, but it slips away. Maybe our premises were all wrong, or we simply happened to be at the wrong place at the wrong time. Then it seems like the rest of our lives follows suit. We are shown just how far we have to fall.

Our ancestors may look back on the passage of peak oil with a similar sense of loss. They might wonder what could have been, if humanity only heeded compassion instead of avarice. Carl Sagan, in his Kermit-the-frog voice, hypothesized that if the superstitious and violent elements of Christianity hadn't risen to the top, we could be voyaging to the stars as we speak.

Thinking about that, I'm sure you could easily find the theme for a story.

Let's explore more. It is hard to imagine what it must have felt like at the turning point of an age, now long gone. What a sense of loss it must have been to see the Library of Alexandria, a cathedral to the best knowledge of that time, pillaged down to scraps and fragments, ancient knowledge lost to a growing darkness that lasted an age. (Sounds like something out of *Lord of the Rings*, doesn't it?)

At the time of its destruction, the Library of Alexandria was overseen by Hypatia, who was a surprising figure in such patriarchal times. She was was reviled as a witch because she wouldn't take a husband, and, probably the worse offense, she dabbled in the dark arts of philosophy, mathematics and science. These were about to be largely written off as occult sorcery for several centuries.

Even in the 16th-17th century, Giordano Bruno was killed for proclaiming the Sun was merely a star, perhaps adrift in the suburbs of the milky way and the Earth just her dark passenger. ("Milky" because of the milk cast off from Hera's tits, I find that amusing.) This was roughly 1000 years after Hypatia had her skin flayed from her body with pottery shards for having the audacity to embrace reason. Quite a learning curve.

We toss off such stories casually, but if you identify your reader with a character, and then have her skin peeled away like the rind of a stubborn fruit with pieces of broken earth, they'll probably take notice. (And wonder why you're such a sadist.) I'm not sure why many of us consider this kind of thing entertainment. Maybe it gives a visceral sense of the extremity of a moment in time, so long ago.

Despite its distance in time, it is not as if we are much further developed as spiritual beings.

Indeed, our spiritual ideas structured many seemingly unrelated cultural institutions. It was maybe only because of Aristotle's view of divinity as the perfect mind that worked behind the Empirical world that the ideas of Classical antiquity could be re-purposed.

Many old ideas were reborn during the Renaissance– what hadn't been burned or buried, at any rate. It was only when a way was found to render these ideas palatable to the biases of the time that science and math could again flourish, this time, when married with industry and war, as the part of a new tradition running out of control as religion did in the previous era. The Renaissance reversed the age of darkness, but it was in some ways merely an amplified echo, a carrier wave dragging ideas kicking and screaming through time. If we pretend that history is a strictly linear process, it is easy to imagine that we are approaching our own dark age as the sine wave crests and falls.

It doesn't matter if that's true or not. Historians might argue about that for a thousand years. A writer can casually toss up their hands and say, "hey, I'm a writer. So. Do you keep any whiskey around here?"

If we look at past instances of systemic collapse, we can find patterns relevant to our fictional explorations.

As a writer of modern myths– let's not fool ourselves, that's what a fiction writer is – we are also untethered from historical necessity. If the record doesn't match our theme, we should feel free to borrow from it as we see fit, and toss what doesn't match our crazed designs as we search for psychological truth. Mythic truth. So, we can see in our past a limitless sea of themes which will be reborn in different forms throughout our collective futures.

We could turn such "darkness" into the theme for a science fiction or fantasy story. We could cast it in a realistic-seeming alternate history. That's purely aesthetic. For instance, the movie *Agora* deals with Hypatia and this idea of a culture's decline into darkness, however, the creative team felt free to actually exercise their creativity.

This idea of the fall from grace can be spun a million ways. Many of us feel deep rage when we think of all that has been lost to the carelessness and ignorance of humanity through time, or even just to the callous indifference, the forgetfulness of death. This can be a great theme for a story, but it's all in what you do with it.

A solid theme and setting based on a mental exercise like this won't assure a good story. That's the job of a writer. I don't think anyone reading this needs a crash course on the craft involved. But a well-paced and crafted novel devoid of a broader theme is an exercise in futility if we are looking to take Zeno on and shoot for the bullseye.

If you don't think of yourself as a writer, consider all the internal writing you've done to help codify and interlink the personal and cultural myths of your life. The two are not so clearly demarcated as we might imagine. You may not write for the entertainment of others, but in all other ways that count, you both receive and transmit myth, changing it, either a little or a lot, before passing it along. Own this, at least to the extent that it owns you.

An arrow *can* reach its mark by progressing in half steps, as all writers know. I'm fairly convinced that is the only way books are written– in defiance of common sense.

Carts And Horses

The Deification of the Brain

James Curcio

We have already considered the noisome gap between that which falls under the purview of science, and what belongs instead to myth. It is a direct result of misconceptions discussed there that we see a constant glut of so-called "science" articles making claims such as "neuro scientists say that evil no longer exists," (Slate article) or "neuroscience versus philosophy, taking aim at free well." (Nature.com article).

Let me use these two articles as an example of what is actually an epidemic that needs immediate and complete overhaul. (Enough of one that research has been done on this topic, see: "Can It Read My Mind?"– What Do the Public and Experts Think of the Current (Mis)Uses of Neuroimaging?)

The Slate article is considerably more egregious than the latter, as it presents a singular interpretation as the only possible answer to a very complicated question that has challenged the best minds throughout our sordid history.

However, both are unified in this particular detail: they depend on a materialist presupposition at the outset and then use this model as a self-evident proof of materialist claims. I know that sounds somewhat abstract, so let's look at the position posed by these articles directly,

Is evil over? Has science finally driven a stake through its dark heart? Or at least emptied the word of useful meaning, reduced the notion of a numinous nonmaterial malevolent force to a glitch in a tangled cluster of neurons, the brain?

Yes, according to many neuroscientists, who are emerging as the new high priests of the secrets of the psyche, explainers of human behavior in general. A phenomenon attested to by a recent torrent of pop-sci brain books with titles like Incognito: The Secret Lives of the Brain. Not secret in most of these works is the disdain for metaphysical evil, which is regarded as an antiquated concept that's done more harm than good. They argue that the time has come to replace such metaphysical terms with physical explanations– malfunctions or malformations in the brain.

Of course, people still commit innumerable bad actions, but the idea that people make conscious decisions to hurt or harm is no longer sustainable, say the new brain scientists. For one thing, there is no such thing as "free will" with which to decide to commit evil. (Like evil, free will is an antiquated concept for most.) Autonomous, conscious decision-making itself may well be an illusion. And thus intentional evil is impossible.

It would seem that for every benefit neuroscience gives us, it puts us back an equal amount when it comes to our sense of personal agency. Or, contrarily, I can stab you in the eye and say my brain made me do it. And since we're all mechanical beings, if my kidneys start to go, I'll just carve yours out of your back.

Granted, society– a meta-machine, if you will– can and should lock me away in either event as a means of self-defense. So functionally, there's no difference.

But functionally there is no difference between determinism and free will to begin with. That's not the point. *This is a misappropriation of science for myth-making.*

The free will vs determinism argument is irrelevant to scientific enterprise, but very relevant to how we look at the world. Philosophy is meta-mythology. Rather than posing an example clothed in the engaging narrative of the specific, it instead looks for the abstract. But make no mistake, we are dealing in mythology. (Or literature, if you prefer.)

Ultimately, one side or the other– free will or determinism– isn't upheld by "discoveries in neuroscience."

Why? The underlying premises of the article are specious on two accounts: idealism vs. materialism and free will vs. determinism. In both cases we're talking about conceptual carts and horses. Attribute "cause" to one side, "effect" to the other; or similarly, "primary" and "secondary." Do you see? *We* are the ones attributing value, imposing hierarchy through our presuppositions.

We are the ones myth-making.

This kind of either/or thinking is easily outmoded by models in both science as well as philosophy the past 50 years, so this isn't a case of neuroscience having outstripped philosophy or the other way around. Rather, it's a case of the article writer trying to paint a picture, and attempting to use science as a cover for some bad literary philosophy.

It is somewhat ironic that both of these arguments are silently penned atop a myth that goes back to Descartes, that old yarn about mind / body dualism. As I said, this way of looking at the world has mostly been done away with as an accurate model, neatly dividing mind and matter. What we have instead is an admittedly more willy-nilly view of consciousness that calls to mind the paradoxical existence of light simultaneously as wave and particle. I would ask that the writers of these articles use modern philosophical models to frame the modern scientific discoveries they're espousing, rather than a framework grounded in the 17th century.

Should we consider light to behave as a wave or a particle? Well, it depends on how you look at it. The same can be said of our minds. (Note that I didn't say "*is* light a wave or a particle." Both of these things are models.)

Is our consciousness intrinsically tied to the electrochemical goo inside our skulls? Yes, it certainly seems that way. Can we thereby reduce all issues to a quantifiable, strictly behaviorist, materialist, (even positivist) science, and finally "solve" *all* philosophical quandaries through scientific measurement? Hardly.

To explain why would take us on a long journey through the history of both the past 100 years in science and philosophy. We might consider some major steps along the way to include the works of Neils Bohr, Ludwig Wittgenstein, Jacques Derrida, Werner Heisenberg (though let's be honest: nobody truly understands quantum mechanics,) and of course Albert Einstein. The questions relevant to this particular inquiry seem simple enough, but they remain as perplexing today as they were in the age of the Ancient Greeks: what is the nature of mind? what is the nature of matter?

Ventures in this direction often lead to semantic arguments. This feels too fanciful for the veneer of cargo cult science. We are no longer concerned with such fluff, the modern consumer of pop science literature clearly wants "hard answers."

Semantic arguments are not necessarily *just* semantic arguments. Our presuppositions about consciousness, how we define it, how we define concepts such as "will" or "freedom," are far more important than neuroscans when deciding whether our actions are "free" or "determined." It is highly probable that our nervous system has made its own determination before we became consciously *aware* of that decision – or so neuroscientists tell me– but that is merely "passing the buck" as they say.

Within the context of the conundrum of consciousness, free will seems merely a footnote. What these articles, and those like them, seem to be proclaiming is actually this: "Philosophy and myth are dead. Long live science."

Few would argue that our consciousness is brought about by brain and nerves, but the question remains, can we have a unified theory of mind and matter, or must we continue to think of carts and horses? Is it our language itself that creates this delineation, which says "my body," as if it was a bio-mechanical walker that my brain is floating in, and within that, a mind. (And within that? It's "turtles all the way down.")

Pop science likes to pretend that we are just around the corner from "answering" such questions, as if they can be answered without posing another framework that needs exploration. The truth is that we've fallen off the wagon, having lost any sense of the intellectual history that has brought us to this point. The cart is speeding off down the road without us.

In the long tradition of wrestling with these questions, we've continually confused the role of myth and the role of science. The nature of mind is not measured, it is explored, just as the realm of experience is not weighed but rather felt.

Richard Feynman made a speech on "cargo cult" science that seems relevant,

I think the educational and psychological studies I mentioned are examples of what I would like to call cargo cult science. In the South Seas there is a cargo cult of people. During the war they saw airplanes land with lots of good materials, and they want the same thing to happen now. So they've arranged to imitate things like runways, to put fires along the sides of the runways, to make a wooden hut for a man to sit in, with two wooden pieces on his head like headphones and bars of bamboo sticking out like antennas– he's the controller– and they wait for the airplanes to land. They're doing everything right. The form is perfect. It looks exactly the way it looked before. But it doesn't work. No airplanes land. So I call these things cargo cult science, because they follow all the apparent precepts and forms of scientific investigation, but they're missing something essential, because the planes don't land.

Of course, the neuroscience that articles such as these are pointing toward are "real" science, so this is even more treacherous ground for the unwary. They are drawing unscientific conclusions from scientific research. This, as I've said before, is the realm of myth– and that is well and good, except for when we fool ourselves into mistaking the metaphor for reality. We are then, in some ways, no different from the fundamentalist Christian that takes the Bible for literal truth.

If an experience or phenomenon can't be rigorously scientifically tested, that doesn't mean it doesn't have some kind of reality to it. As we have seen, there are elements of our experience– and thus, our world as well– that don't parse particularly well into the scientific method. They either can't be falsified, or they can't be repeated, or they can't in some other way be parsed in an empirical, iterative model. That is perfectly fine. If we had less cultural pressure to "science-ize" everything, there would also be less psuedo-science, fewer cargo cults.

A central part of Karl Popper's project is figuring out how to draw the line between science and pseudo-science. The big difference Popper identifies between science and pseudo-science is a difference in attitude. While a pseudo-science is set up to look for evidence that supports its claims, Popper says, a science is set up to challenge its claims and look for evidence that might prove it false. In other words, pseudo-science seeks confirmations and science seeks falsifications.

There is a corresponding difference that Popper sees in the form of the claims made by sciences and pseudo-sciences: Scientific claims are falsifiable – that is, they are claims where you could set out what observable outcomes would be impossible if the claim were true – while pseudo-scientific claims fit with any imaginable set of observable outcomes. What this means is that you could do a test that shows a scientific claim to be false, but no conceivable test could show a pseudo-scientific claim to be false. Sciences are testable, pseudo-sciences are not. **"Drawing The Line Between Science and Psuedo-Science," Scientific American.**

If we posit the premise "we are biological robots," from that we can– no, must– build a myth. But whether we are "just" biological robots, or whether life is a magical thing, that falls to the simple aesthetics of the myth we're constructing.

This is where our myths begin– which is why I feel such fire in regard to getting these ideas out there to you. I recognize that most people don't understand the importance or relevance of immanent mythology. Hopefully our work these past few years– and in the coming years– will make that clear enough that many others will take up the work, as they are in other disciplines that are gradually becoming aware of the greatest mystery of all: the narrative is not an afterthought. The narrative is everything.

Getting Fucked Senseless:

Myth Against Myth

Rowan Tepper

Dianus was the pseudonym under which Georges Bataille published the first part of *Guilty*, which has recently been published in a new translation by Stuart Kendall on SUNY Press, under the title *Friendship*, in April 1940. In an abandoned draft for an introduction to the second edition, Bataille wrote that *Friendship* had a sacred– which is also to say ambivalent (as Bataille was influenced by Durkheim)– character.

Indeed, the pseudonym itself suggests as much, as the name is "that of a great Latin god, Janus, or Dianus," and refers to the "King of the Wood," the priest of Diana at Nemi– a position attained by virtue of a crime; it was necessary to kill one's predecessor in order to take his place. Finally, the name can also be read as a contraction of *Dieu* and *anus* (pardon my French): "God's asshole," as the name of the author of Story of the Eye, Lord Auch less directly means: "God to the shithouse"– which suits the priestly nature of Dianus– or, "That asshole, God."

An earlier version had included an additional note attributed to Dianus:

> *later, quickly, all that will remain of us will be an absent memory of our inability to imagine this moment which, henceforth, we will have surpassed: this unimaginable world into which I cannot enter other than by refusing to imagine it, laughing at myself, repudiating it... What does this (book) mean? Would it already be for human intelligence what this world that shatters it is? A betrayal of man by the world, or a betrayal of the world by man? ...Unhappy, am I not in each point similar to you, complicit with each blunder?* (164-5)

What produces the illusion, the myth of transcendence? It is the capacity to think in terms of beings, the possibility of naming, of objectifying reality, and in the Sartrean version, *women*. His womanizing was consonant with his insistence on transcendence. As subject, he could not avoid objectifying them.

To do otherwise would have been in bad faith. It is also a matter of unification, and as Bataille wrote in the unpublished "philosophical epilogue" to his book *On Nietzsche*,

...it is the possibility of being named that is decisive... I call being (a being) a movement that closes in upon itself, unifying limited elements." The act of naming makes a given unity/singularity into a being, a being is inasmuch as it can be distinguished from every other being of its kind. The simplest components of the material world, elementary particles, such as atoms, molecules, etc, "cannot be considered as beings in that one cannot name this atom here, that molecule there. [But] a cell, an animal, a colony or animal society are beings. (OC VI 443)

In publishing *Friendship* under the pseudonym Dianus, and then publishing *Guilty* and *The Impossible* pretending to be the editor of the posthumous notes of Dianus– who, it is discovered in the second part of *The Impossible*, committed suicide– and the notes of one Monsignor Alpha, Bataille distinguishes two existences immanent in himself, in every individuated self, every being.

The ensuing philosophical tragicomedy culminates with an evocation of Orestes– a figure of poetry, of mythology, and also the "protagonist" of Sartre's play *The Flies*– who, in one version of the myth of the Tauric Diana, "whose priest at Nemi was the King of the Wood," instituted the priesthood when he fled to the lake at Nemi seeking absolution for a murder." Dianus thus serves as the persona of the counterpart of the existentialist hero of tragic freedom found in Sartre's retelling of the Orestes myth.

The myth of transcendence is everywhere, throughout the history of philosophy, and even more so, theology. It is behind the myth of the subject, of the free, autonomous individual, and it was the dominant myth of Enlightenment philosophy and the historical-social-political concepts and practices in Modernity. The accomplishment of the culmination of Idealism in Hegel was that he made transcendence into the already-achieved culmination of the dialectical processes of history. With the attainment of "Absolute Spirit" by the vanguard, the European bourgeoisie at the height of the German Enlightenment, the dialectic came to a halt, to a conclusion: transcendence was thereby transformed into an immanent myth.

It is not at all surprising that both the analytic and phenomenological-existential Continental philosophical traditions fundamentally presuppose transcendence whether or not the subject opposed to the object is spoken of plainly or disguised by the jargon of authenticity. It follows that transcendence is even more than what Hans Blumenberg calls an "absolute myth," it is the meta-myth of the West and the principle of our alienation– from others and from ourselves. Dianus and the cast of the melodrama that unfolds in the play of pseudonyms and that is staged in *The Impossible*, in which the suicidal pseudonym himself stars as narrator, evoke "the obscure region close to phenomenologists," Bataille's "objectivity": the immanence that life truly is.

It is myth against myth. Myth as comedy against the mythical tragedy of the free, autonomous and incurably lonely self.

Life is a Tragicomedy. Taken seriously, life is a tragedy, but beyond seriousness the tragic devolves into senseless laughter. Suppose that Hamlet interrupts the dying speech of Laertes saying: "Ha! I've spent many years working up an immunity..." It's inconceivable.

Love is tragic, sex on the other hand– and let's be honest with ourselves– is fucking funny. What's more: we lose our sense of existing as individuals with names while fucking. We don't analyze, we don't "make sense," if we're lucky we end up fucked senseless: Whether it be sex, the sacred, or DMT, there are moments during which immanence is felt and we can only laugh at the phrase "hell is other people." It is the same with laughter, anguish and ecstasy, and this senseless loss of self is the very possibility and instantiation– when shared– of communication and the sacred friendship of the opening pages of *Guilty*.

Toasters, Bladerunner and Schizophrenia:

PKD & Gnostic Agnosticism

Mr. VI

Do you know who you are, and can you honestly say your awareness encompasses the whole of the biomechanical system which is you-as an organism? May you be aware of the functioning of each organ; the pulsing of the heart, the filtering of the liver and kidneys, or the electrical crackle in your own brain?

Do you sing the body electric?

They say it's bad to ask questions of your audience. It's disruptive; breaks the flow, tears at the weave and begins to fray the threads by which they draw themselves into your narrative. But what better way to examine, to dig underneath the skin?

We're all skin-jobs. That's the derogatory term for Replicants in Ridley Scott's seminal film *Bladerunner*, just as 'Toaster' is used for Cylons in *Battlestar:Galactica*.

Actually, this whole article was inspired by Edward James Olmos live-tweeting Bladerunner the other Sunday:

> @edwardjolmos: #movienighttweet *it all came from this film... BSG skinjobs... replicants.... thus toasters...*

Behind both epithets lies the notion of falsity, of facsimile. In both narratives, we are presented with the notion that there are those who look like us, but are not like us. In Bladerunner, we are left with Deckard's humanity as an ambiguous question, while in BS:G the hybridization and shift into flesh leaves us with the possibility that the markers of "humanity" are perhaps not so clear-cut as we would like to believe.

Bladerunner uses a test known as the Voight-Kampff to test empathetic responses – and if those responses are off, 'retirement' is not far away. The film itself is an adaptation of Philip K. Dick's novel, *Do Androids Dream of Electric Sheep*, and it's no secret that I'm a total and utter Dick-head.

In fact, anyone with an interest in philosophy, storytelling, myth and SF should be one too. Just look at the following:

I am a fictionalizing philosopher, not a novelist; my novel & story-writing ability is employed as a means to formulate my perception. The core of my writing is not art but truth. Thus what I tell is the truth, yet I can do nothing to alleviate it, either by deed or explanation. Yet this seems somehow to help a certain kind of sensitive troubled person, for whom I speak. I think I understand the common ingredient in those whom my writing helps: they cannot or will not blunt their own intimations about the irrational, mysterious nature of reality, &, for them, my corpus is one long ratiocination regarding this inexplicable reality, an integration & presentation, analysis & response & personal history. **Philip K. Dick**

In 1974, Dick had a series of mystical experiences which influenced his writing from then on, exploring his own version of Gnosticism. For us, it's the Gnostic view combined with schizophrenia that's interesting.

In *Schizophrenia and The Book of Changes* he writes:

What distinguishes schizophrenic existence from that which the rest of us like to imagine we enjoy is the element of time. The schizophrenic is having it all now, whether he wants it or not; the whole can of film has descended on him, whereas we watch it progress frame by frame.

This, combined with the Gnostic idea that the world is a creation of the demiurge, which presupposes itself as sole Creator, can be seen in a rather strange light: that reality as we know it is defined by mediated perception.

It's our perception which ascribes the notion of "real" in its sense of "false" to a thing, and our perception is a direct, inextricable product of our sensory organs. The flesh, the body, is the only reality we know, and indeed can know.

In the words of Roy Batty, leader of the Replicants:

I've done questionable things [...] Nothing the god of biomechanics wouldn't let you into Heaven for.

Whereas the Gnostics sought to escape the creation of the demiurge, seeking a "true" reality, the slogan of the Replicant manufacturer "More Human Than Human" seems eerily prescient. Despite our scientific knowledge, the mechanics of existence still elude us.

To be sure, analysis and the scientific method have provided us with an understanding of the parts of the body, of the reality-factory which is us. We can piece together the frames in an attempt to gain some sense of the plot, but the totality of the film escapes us.

Who knows what plot-twists are concealed? What pieces of foreshadowing are we focusing on as-themselves, rather than as part of the whole narrative?

So much is carried out behind the scenes of our awareness, it's as if we're watching a rough-cut. Our idea of humanness is based upon what we perceive as human, what we perceive of ourselves in others; this is the empathic echo– the Voight-Kampff.

And yet, as the New Scientist points out, nothing is as it seems, and our memories are subject to flux. We have memory 'implants' as much as the Replicants do; we're not all biologists or genetic engineers, but we still manufacture our pasts and create futures – we're some kind of genus of strange factories.

Perception even defines the "now":

You're reading this book, experiencing these words, dimly aware of noises around you or in the other room, but weren't experiencing them until the words led you to consider the place you currently occupy, in greater detail, were you?

Imagine what it would be like if the moments of your perception began to blur; if the frames start beginning to bleed and an oozing tide of imagery and sensation slams into you like a tsunami and you're drowning in reality itself?

Sweeping you away, uprooting fundamentals, slamming you through things that were seemingly solid; walls of skin and bone pierced by the world, sending you backward to swallow that initial cry of birth.

The trauma of your world expelling you; from timeless darkness with its endless heartbeat rhythms, into the absence of blood-heat as the chill settles around you, with light stabbing your eyes like shards of frosted, jagged glass; myriad new sensations as lungs take in their first breath.

In time, most of us wall that experience away; we either forget or attempt to parse overloads, so that they become still images.

Welcome to the world, to the first Outside.

We splice together the frames, or leave whole chunks on the cutting room floor, because otherwise we'd still be screaming.

Like mad people.

Over-perception then; the realm of the supposedly *insane*. Perception is the realm of the sane, a limitation, a demarcation; without the separation and division, it all becomes nonsensical. There must be an inside and outside.

So *they* say.

The alternative terrified the Gnostics, and still terrifies the majority of people. That the dividing is a bulwark from terror is easily seen; the notion of order is one of contour and boundary. The idea that we are all Inside– that there is no escape from everything– inmates in our own Black Iron Prison, can and does inspire paranoia and fear.

Yet, that's the hard Agnostic Gnosticism of it. We're never able to know beyond our senses. Perception is merely modulation of sensory data. If we stick to frame-by-frame, acting out of fear, it means the film ends. So:

We can't even tell if we're Replicants. Can't trust our memories, or our assumptions, or our senses. All we have is now, this moment, and even that is being filtered by our imagined pasts and futures.

> *I've seen things you people wouldn't believe. Attack ships on fire off the shoulder of Orion. I've watched C-beams glitter in the dark near the Tannhauser Gate. All those moments will be lost in time, like tears in the rain. Time to die.* **Blade Runner.**

Isn't that extraordinarily fun?

Living Your Myth

James Curcio

This article was first published, with some variation, in *The Immanence of Myth*

(Weaponized, August 2011).

To die for an idea is stupid, people say. Ideas aren't *real*.

Nowadays, the posture of choice is disengagement. Sure, we'll discuss ideas. Especially if it has any hope of getting us laid. But commitment to an idea or an ideal is so... *passe*. That was something that died with the 20th century, along with a lot of things that we can happily say we've left to rot in the past. Intellectual is a synonym with ineffectual. Art is a pretense by definition. The highest art now is art that makes fun of itself, or so says the co-creator of just such a piece.

Well, I've talked a great deal on ModernMythology.net about the ways that ideas-as-myths are living as much as we are. The ways that myths enter into the world, enter into "reality," especially through our actions. The ways they real-ize beliefs, and how we re-ify the world through them.

Sounds like a lot of bullshit *ideas* to me.

A writer deals in words. Words symbolize ideas. They can evoke emotions. But what's in a word, really? When is it time for action, and what is that action?

What is the greatest act a person can make? Is it the greatest sacrifice? And how many of you think your ideas are worth dying for? Certainly the suicide bomber has been convinced of this. We look away in discomfort or snub our noses at such fanatics. Mostly, I'd say, rightly so. They've been duped. They've been sold a unicorn and paid for it with flesh blood and mortar, and not all of it was theirs to sacrifice.

But there's another side to this posture of disengagement and apathy. It turns us to good cattle, good consumers, good slaves who do our master's bidding because it is easier that way, easier than challenging and possibly facing death as the repercussion of our actions. Maybe this was the future that Yukio Mishima saw for his dying Empire; a future so bereft of honor and dignity that the only thing he could do in response was shove a blade through his innards. The death of a warrior, not a writer. His suicide could then be seen as a final transformation: writer into warrior, thinker into actor. But this transformation is only complete when it resonates with a culture, when those ripples reach outwards across the years, transform entire civilizations. We all know the power of a martyr.

This was not Mishima's fate. He was a man in so many ways out of step with his time, a relic. To mix metaphors, if a man can become a metaphor, he was the final gasp of a dying mythology. The modern narrative on suicide, even in Japan, is not what it was. To the West, his was the death of a coward. We even sigh sadly at the thought of Hunter S Thompson blowing his brains out, a sound not unlike a book dropping heavily to the floor, or so said his son Juan. What poetry, the final sound for a writer to make. A book falling to the floor. Or perhaps Juan was doing a little myth-making of his own.

We say: they did it before their time. We say: they had no right. And how possessive of us, to think that we own a person that it is their duty to stick around and churn out material for us until our absentee landlord God finally pulls the plug? Maybe Hunter's wife or son gets to say he had no right, or at least, you son of a bitch. You left us here because you were selfish.

> Does she feel she failed him? "Oh, I did. The job of a wife is to protect your husband when there are dark forces around, or when he is feeling dark and depressed. I failed at it."

> The biggest problem was his health; after an operation on his back, Thompson fell over and broke a leg while on a faintly improbable assignment to cover the Honolulu marathon. This reignited the back problems and raised the spectre of yet another operation– which he dreaded.

> "But he had so much more work ahead of him. He was so much fun," says Anita. Still in thrall to him, despite all the arguments, she has just written a book called The Gonzo Way– a thoroughly readable account of Thompson's philosophy and final years.

> "The best thing about our marriage was that it was like being married to a teenage girl trapped in the body of an elderly dope fiend," says Anita. "Which was also the hardest thing about our marriage."

> She sighs and wells up again: "As of January 1 this year, I thought I'd start dating again. But I miss him. I've realised it's going to be a challenge finding anything interesting in life after his death. But the last thing he would want me to do is to spend the rest of my days simply mourning."

> She's right. It's not the Gonzo Way. **Times Online Article**

I could be wrong myself, but I think *they* got it wrong. I think this is masking the fact that he didn't have much left in him, that his story was over. That his story had been done for a little while. He alluded to this in the note he left.

He could've stuck around for his wife. Maybe he should have. But for us, the public? We have no right to ask that of him. Hunter, Mishima, anyone that said: "it is time." Let them be the author of their lives. And let them realize that when you hit return on that final sentence, there are no do-overs. There is no editorial review. That. Is. It.

What right do any of us have, if not to choose how and when we leave this life? We did not choose to come here. So many things in our lives– most things– appear to be in our control but actually are not. It is one of the most predominant myths of the West, these days. Self empowerment. You control your destiny!

Here's a little wake up call. We control nearly nothing. We are links in a chain, cells in a body, accidents in a cosmic equation. Gods of our inner worlds, yes, but when we sit down at the table with the board of directors, do we get to make demands? No. We don't. Because reality is that which does not go away when we cease to believe in it. (Or so said Phillip K. Dick.)

I'd like to turn back to Yukio Mishima. Are you familiar with him? He was, by the time of his death, a celebrated, famous author. I've only read fragments of his writing. It is full of emotionally reserved or stunted men. The characters are, frankly, less interesting than he himself was, although his protagonists all seem to be foils for himself anyhow, as is often the case. At least Hunter made us laugh.

But Mishima was also a genius, and it wasn't just because of his craftsmanship with the pen. It was because, in his own way, he faced this conflict between the word and reality, and when it came to it, he didn't back down. It was an unyielding, possibly obsessive commitment to the narrative he had build that eventually guided the blade that killed him.

The comedy in this tragedy was that it meant nothing. He killed himself because the soldiers, who were meant to be roused by the speech he made after barricading himself in with the Tatenokai, merely laughed at him. Their laughter must have rung in his ears like the jests of the schoolboys who snidely called him "poet," who teased him so mercilessly that he had to hide his aspirations as a writer. Later in life, nominated to be a Nobel Laureate, and still the punchline of a joke. He spent years weight training, focusing on his body. Sun and Steel. Still he was just the poet. There was nothing to do but die honorably, and that too was a failure. His second could not perform his deed, and Koga had to step in and behead them both.

John-Ivan Palmer began a search, years after their ritual suicide, to track down Koga. To ask the questions that no one was asking, beginning with: why did no one speak to Koga? Why was the speculation about Mishima's death so fixated on odd miscellanea like his sublimated (or not so sublimated) homosexuality? Can we look past our bias about suicide and see how, at least as an author, an author of his own life, he concluded the story in the only way, ultimately, that it could be concluded? This too is a part of living our myth.

In the end, John-Ivan Palmer never reached Koga directly. This may have been because he didn't ultimately follow the right channels. But it could also be for a more poetic reason. All he got was a phone call, signifying silence. Read this:

That night my phone rang at 3 a.m., but when I picked it up I heard only background noise, like traffic. Otherwise silence. Twenty minutes later the phone rang a second time, and there was a different kind of background noise in the silence. Twenty minutes after that the phone rang a third time and there was yet a third kind of silence. Now insomnia kicked in as my mind came up with more questions.

In Japanese, unlike English, there exists an onomatopoeic sound for absolute silence. You sometimes see it in Japanese comic books (manga) where there are so many words that resemble the sound they denote that special English translators have been hired separately to translate them. The Japanese word for silence is "sin," pronounced more or less like "sheeeen..." with the sound trailing off at the end. Like "whoosh" is the sound of a sword cutting through the air, and "gurgle" is the sound of blood spurting out the neck hole, "sin" is the "sound" afterward, when all is done, the bodies removed, everyone gone home, and only the silence remains.

Did the silence of those phone calls represent a Zen answer, one each from Hiroyasu Koga, Masayoshi Koga, and Masahiro Ogawa, or did all three calls come from Koga himself? Or was it merely three different wrong numbers in the middle of the night that just happened to be spaced exactly 20 minutes apart, disturbing my sleep by reminding me, reminding me, reminding me?

That silence could be the sound of our resignation. Not blood spurting from a wound. Just the whimper of a world sucking sustenance though tubes. No bang. No surprises.

Are there ideas that are so tightly wound into your myth that you are willing to die for them? If not, does that make you stronger for carrying out the story past the final chapter, or does it simply make you like the actor who, after the final curtain call, stands on the stage, and repeats his lines over and over in some delusional hope that the curtain will rise again?

Why is it so important *how* they died? We are interested because of how they got there, yet we fixate on the end. Thus we see our teleological obsession, our fixation on ends; the culmination, finish, or goal, the idealized future, and also the ends to means.

This future-fixation, as I discussed in *The Immanence of Myth,* was dealt with in an essay by Alan Dundes. I won't repeat the ideas I presented there, though I suggest you pick up our book.

But I do want to direct our gaze towards living rather than dying, for those who might interpret what I said as advocacy of suicide. There are, maybe, many people this world could use less of. The likes of Hunter S Thompson and Yukio Mishima are not amongst them.

Maybe the literary nature of the suicides of authors, we can for instance add Hemingway to this list, should not be especially surprising. As every story, we believe, must have a beginning middle and end.

If we are so committed to a particular identity, or if our body simply will no longer bear us forward into a new story, then that end will be literal.

But what about this identification with character? Can we transcend it? What is suicide but the most extreme act of ego transcendence of which we are capable?

In a 1978 BBC interview, Hunter S Thompson said,

> I'm never sure which one people expect me to be. Very often, they conflict– most often, as a matter of fact. ...I'm leading a normal life and right along side me there is this myth, and it is growing and mushrooming and getting more and more warped. When I get invited to, say, speak at universities, I'm not sure if they are inviting Duke or Thompson. I'm not sure who to be.

We are prone to say someone "has a big ego," that they are "full of themselves," and that someone is too connected to their ego if they think that they must literally die to move beyond a persona that has outlived its usefulness, or its place.

Maybe we should look a bit more at what we're actually talking about here. People aren't inherently more or less "deep" by nature, though some are prone to introspection, some are prone to vanity, etc. It is in the act that our spiritual wealth or bankruptcy becomes evident. The "play is the thing," yes?

In my experience, the people we often accuse of having a "big ego" simply can't see under their own surface, they are opaque to themselves. The "big" ego is really one that has become opaque, either to the outside or to itself. We might also mistake persona for ego, or use them interchangeably, and identify with beliefs and ideas to such an extent that they become like our second skin.

I think that's where the appearance of shallowness arises from. Opacity makes the ego "small," in a sense; fixed, hungry and confused. I believe this can work both ways, too. When we are ourselves more frightened or scared by environmental factors, for instance, our ego itself seems to close in, to become opaque and fixate on those stressors until they are dealt with. If they are not, or cannot be, this fixation can become neurotic.

None of this is a matter of size, metaphorical or otherwise. The ego of a Zen master, say, is *huge,* like the broad peripheral vision that takes in the whole sunset. It encompasses far more than the small ego that clings to trinkets, or which has focused in because of approaching danger. What a *small* ego, to think that it is made more illustrious because its flesh puppet wears an expensive gold watch. Martial arts rewire our bodies to flow rather than be trapped by stress that might otherwise lock up or fixate the mind.

But anyone who would ever go by "teacher" "master" etc and simultaneously claim to be entirely without ego... well, that's just a little bit absurd. The teachers that claim they have transcended ego and through that "know reality" are the ones we should be especially wary of.

Again, the issue isn't the ego, but rather its opacity or transparency. In other words, where do our thoughts or ideas *stop*, where do they cluster and bunch up and fixate, against what barrier do we bang ourselves bloody, what skin? Where does our center of concern fall? What fears and desires obsess us?

We don't need to annihilate our fears or desires, but we can see our ego outlined in the contours of them. If our consciousness is fixated on what kind of clothes we're wearing, or what kind of clothes someone else is wearing, that's also the focus of our ongoing meditation. Meditation after all is just the act of making ones self more conscious of consciousness. It's happening all the time, not just when you're doing zazen, asana, or pranayama.

Wherever we are at right now, not where we are *trying* to be, is the focus of our ego. I think that's why people call something or someone "shallow"– that metaphor represents something right? Something is "shallow" or "deep"? Why is *depth* the natural dimension to employ in this metaphor? There seems to be something lurking in this metaphor: If you've got water with light shining into it, how deep does that light penetrate? The water itself goes "all the way down," whether or not the light penetrates a mere inch or for miles. Life spent billions of years evolving to a state where it could become aware of itself, God created us so we could know the creation, but if you're stuck worrying obsessively about if your dress makes you look fat, you probably missed it.

Maybe we mean several different things when we say "ego." It may refer to a continuum of self-concept pertaining both to persona (self concept) and ego (that which perceives). A false dualism to be sure. Or it may refer to the *concept* of pure perception underlying recognition of self within sense data, the imagined ghost in the machine.

If we grant the ego– the "unstruck sound," the inner voice at once thinking and hearing "I"– any existence at all, paradox and infinite regress abounds. Removing it from the equation, on the other hand, seems unsatisfying. The ground of being is shrouded in uncertainty. When we act, suddenly that ground is far more solid. Maybe this shows a linkage between immanence and the act rather than the reflection or abstraction; but immanence seems to reach out to enfold the numinous as well. Can it grasp it? Embody it?

It would seem that the ego is not a *thing* in the world. That awareness isn't contained within the sense impressions, thoughts etc. It appears to give existence to them by being aware of them without being of them (grounded in them.)

What I am talking about is a metaphysical concept we have constructed to think of ourselves (... thinking of ourselves thinking of ourselves thinking of ourselves ...) The Transcendental Ego. If all we need to transcend is philosophical concepts, then many Americans are Buddhas.

This is the nihilistic, reductionist interpretation of Existentialism, of course. The point made by nearly every thinker attached to that label, at one time or another, is that it is in our embodied acts that being resides. We have an existence as a form of being, or we'd like to think we do, but that ego only expresses itself in its effects upon the outside world– in action. Though existentialism is a vague term, it still represents a fundamental shift in awareness: that the internal "I" is– contrary to the thinking of most pre WWII philosophy– an illusion of some kind, or at least unknowable because it has no actual presence in the world. It is "Nothing."

So, let's consider transcendence in this context. There are many Zen metaphors that speak of making the mind clear and undisturbed, like a mountain lake reflecting the moon. (And moonlight itself is, of course, just reflected light.) This does not mean anything need be transcended. It means just what it says: make yourself transparent enough that you can see *through* to so much beauty. Get out of the way of yourself.

Let me repeat: nothing needs to be transcended. Everything is immanent.

My feelings about transcendence and ego aren't some kind of resentment. Here's the danger with the ego transcendence, guru racket: these terms are used to manipulate and dupe people. All myths can be used to this purpose, resulting in many behaviors, including suicide.

Immanence is usually seen as the dialectical opposite of transcendence. I have come to see it as a solution to the *problem* of transcendence, or even the problem which the idea of transcendence itself seeks to resolve. This problem is: should we "transcend" what we define as the negative, or should we take it as "immanent," that is, seek the sacred *in* life?

I realize this may seem incredibly theoretical to some of you. This ceases to be armchair philosophy the moment we can make the jump and realize that our myths determine how we parse the world, and how we behave within it. Remember what I said about suicide bombers. Aside from metaphysical, extensive thinking, consciousness can only be known so long as it is conscious of some object.

So, all of these terms– "transcendent," "immanent," etc.– pose problems of psychological or spiritual *orientation*. To transcend is to move past or avoid, to make immanent is to cease resisting but rather to embrace. If you take an entirely materialist perspective of the world, these are not problems that would even occur to you. If you are more inward-facing in your psychological makeup, certainly if you are more spiritual, then these problems will likely seem more common sense.

The philosophy we outline in the *Immanence of Myth* is, among other things, opposed to the ideas of transcendence and the absolute, but only to the extent that they are used to block out immanence, manifestation, and actual experience. The origin of this idea, at least to my thinking, didn't originate with Heidegger, but it still meshes well enough with Being-in-the-world,

> *Heidegger learned from Husserl but made phenomenological inquiry into a more passive process in which the philosopher allows the phenomenon to speak for itself. In Greek, phenomenon means "that which will reveal itself," but it will reveal itself only when we listen attentively after freeing ourselves from preconceptions. While Husserl had not attempted to uproot Cartesian thinking, Heidegger insists that the central fact of human experience is Being-in-the-world. The observing ego is not separate from the observed world of objects and landscapes. Existence means standing outside oneself: Being is not encapsulated within the skin but spreads over the field of vision, which is a field of Being– Dasien, (literally, "being there.")*
> **Sartre: A Biography, Hayman.**

When people say "they have transcended their ego" I tend to raise an eyebrow and give them a bit of a wide berth until I see what exactly they mean by that. It makes me uneasy, because it means one of two things, and from where I am standing, one of them is not good.

The first seems progressive, radical. They are engaged in an evolutionary act, "shooting the moon," and seeking to grasp at the immanent particulars of their life, to exceed, and excel. They realize that their "self" is just a useful fiction, that their life is a narrative, for all its pains and trials. And yet, by virtue of being alive, they will never actually *transcend* ego. The moment it enters the world, ego becomes myth, but that which it represents is a precondition of self-consciousness. Still, I can get behind this kind of "ego transcendence." Maybe "transcendence" is the wrong word to use, as I just explained.

The *Book of Serenity* (translated by Thomas Cleary, Lindisfarne 1990) case 91: "Nanquan's Peony," deals with this quandary,

> *An old koan asks, "How can you get a goose out of a bottle?" We're asked to imagine that a baby gosling was placed inside one of those big glass bottles with a little opening that you see model ships in, and raised inside, until now it is full grown and can no longer fit through the neck of the bottle. How can you get the goose out of the bottle?*

It's actually a frightening image when we think about what an artificial, cramped and constricted life that poor goose must lead in there, and how unimaginable a life of freedom must be to an animal raised under such conditions. A court official named Lu Geng asks Nanquan (Nan-ch'uan) how to get the goose out of the bottle. Since Lu Geng, in the main part of the case, introduces himself to Nan-ch'uan by reciting someone else's words, I'd guess that the problem of the goose and the bottle was also already a very old, well-known riddle and Lu Geng is testing the master to see what he will make of it. Nan-ch'uan calls "Sir!" and Lu Geng immediately responds, "Yes?" Nan-ch'uan said "It's out." **OrdinaryMind.com**

But from this arises the second possibility: The goose stuck in the bottle that thinks it's free. If someone has really "transcended," why would they *proclaim* their transcendence? It is not a good omen. The Boddhisatva's compassion-as-motivation seems like a cheap excuse on someone covered in chest hair and gold chains. How did ego transcendence become a core doctrine of the self-help movement? Why do you want me to give you $19.95 to help me transcend my ego? Watch footage of Adi Da speak. Pay attention to his rhetoric. Listen to the hushed "oohs" and "aahs" of the audience, and the shift he makes when he begins speaking as the voice of God, that which knows what everything is.

This is "transcending ego"?

The closest I can imagine to true transcendence would be the mythic old Taoist sage, a Lao Tzu, wandering the mountains. (Lao Tzu only means "old man," or "elder teacher.") Or perhaps a Sufi, living with the common folk, but not of them. To be true to its own tenets, it is almost a wonder that Taoism ever became an -ism. Such a Taoist sage would have no desire to start a cult of any kind.

If we say that Ego is the center of the self, the Pole-star of the internal "I," or even a vague sense which travels through our lives and says "me," then we see that it is not something that need be transcended. Why look down on that? Why should we? Doesn't it originate from the same part in us that creates Gods that shame us into relinquishing pleasure?

Be proud of yourself, but not so proud that you delude yourself. Go easier on yourself. Work harder. But also remember that you're a work-in-progress, a quick sketch that'll one day go forgotten in the wastebasket.

Those are things an ego can do, just as much as it can fixate on wealth or lead us to kill a friend for a grilled cheese sandwich. Are either of those bad? It would seem that is an ethical question, not a metaphysical one. The posture of ego transcendence may just be a matter of taste or fashion, a way of distinguishing one's self, which clearly is a function of the ego.

The zero point of death can give us closure on this matter by providing an interesting counterpoint to the ego itself. Death as a moment nullifies the meaning of time. From the vantage point of the end of our history, it matters little if we die tomorrow or in one hundred years. Time is reduced to an n-dimensional space, like a black hole. Or at least that will suffice as a metaphor.

From the vantage point of the present, and from the perspective of our immersion in narratives, it matters very much if we die in one hundred years or tomorrow. And of course, from the outside, all that survives and bridges the gap between life and death is the myth. After the point of death, the ego is no more. Only the myth lives on, now freed of its tethers.

To die for the myth is to live only for the Other; there's an oddly selfless element to the end-point of a suicide like Mishima's. To live for one's self is the real paradox in which we must live our myth and balance that with the unembodied interior life that is a reflection of pure experience. The ego itself could also best be represented by a black hole, an aberration that is only known by the way it distorts all that wanders too near to its event horizon. Though in the case of ego the force at work is myth, not gravity. Of the interior of the ego and the zero point of death we must by all necessity be stricken deaf and dumb. Nothing can escape this paradox– a voice crying out that is only heard when we, its double, mimic that ephemeral gesture.

To end at the beginning, we talked about Yukio Mishima's suicide. Some might see such an act of *Seppuku* as something beyond any moral consideration, an act of transcendence. However, it was the absolute fixation of the ego upon this narrative that demanded its own head be cut off.

You see? We've made Yukio Mishima into a symbol. Yukio Mishima is a pen name by the way, an implied double, an *it*. The name of the man was Kimitake Hiraoka, but his double demanded that he die.

Is this the same with Hunter? I don't think we'll ever know.

How will it be for us? What is our "character"? What does *it* demand? Is it more virtuous to adhere to those demands, to grasp them firmly with both hands and "love them violently," (like Charlie Sheen, or God willing, *not* like him) or to transcend them? That's for all of us to determine. Virtue is another problem for us to contend with in our own way, with our own myths, not to foist upon one another at the end of a sword.

Asking these questions alone is not living your myth. But it can be a good first step.

Incunabula I

Afragility, Twitter, and Embodying Myth

Mr. VI

I personally don't suffer with the problem that Hunter S. Thompson did, the problem which he elucidated in the 1978 BBC documentary, and James recalled in his piece on "Living Your Myth":

> *I'm never sure which one people expect me to be. Very often, they conflict– most often, as a matter of fact. ...I'm leading a normal life and right along side me there is this myth, and it is growing and mushrooming and getting more and more warped. When I get invited to, say, speak at universities, I'm not sure if they are inviting Duke or Thompson. I'm not sure who to be.*

There is no conflict between the myth and reality for me. The Roman numerals which make up **VI** are as much a signifier of my self-hood as the name I was given at birth. Gonzo is the insertion of self into the narrative– the breaking of the notion of objectivity. The author *goes native*, becoming a native of the text or medium.

Native has its roots in natal, relating inextricably to birth and innateness. There is only a conflict if you were ever born somewhere else; the ontological and cultural tensions induce a kind of schizoid existence, a double life, like Clark Kent and Superman or Bruce Wayne and Batman. We've all read enough comics or seen enough of the films and other media to realise that this tension is manufactured by the environment we're in.

Clark Kent and Bruce Wayne are masks. Batman and Superman are the faces behind those masks. Those faces are the real identities, and they are made of myth, born of it. In *Immanence of Myth* James and I talk a great deal about the body, the corpus of myth as living flesh.

Whether it be the twilight world of cannibalism, butchery, or simply eating, fucking and dying, the reasons for such discussions are horrifically simple:

Our bodies, these flesh and blood machines, by their creaking, groaning, pounding and pulsing, are our method of experiencing the universe, and they are the only one we will ever have. The concept of "experience" is rendered not only impossible but also incoherent without a body.

Going native, becoming part of the narrative; this requires that you become myth. It is in a sense, a second birth, a second Nativity– to become the *"rough beast that slouches toward Bethlehem to be born."*

The body becomes the text, the medium. That is when you have become a native, when your very flesh has been juiced with myth, suffused with and marinaded in it.

It may sound insane, to aim to become a living being composed solely of myth; a thing of dream and nebulous, quixotic creative potential. After all, if there is no dividing line between fiction and reality, one is insane, no?

Except, there's things like this, where fictional characters tweet supportive messages to the people of Japan:

In light of the recent tsunami in Japan, a twitter account has recently surfaced with encouraging comments from previous heroes on tokusatsu shows such as Ultraman, Super Sentai and Kamen Rider. *Tokusatsu* means "special filming," of the like seen in Godzilla movies or Power Rangers for those of us not up on Japanese culture. Miraculous effects.

This isn't some mystical becoming-myth. No, it's an attempt to help people parse the enormity of a catastrophe. This is an attempt to give people hope. And it's happening right now, in a so-called 'rational' age. Seriously, am I the only one seeing the connections here? Godzilla and fellow mythic monsters serve a need that goes way beyond rationality.

Because the tension between reality and fiction is manufactured in an attempt to avoid acknowledging the fact that the *majority* of existence has fictive qualities; that apparently fundamental things are actually agreed upon fictions.

In many contexts, the mythic is seen as exterior– the Otherland, the Outside or perhaps some transcendent realm. It can also be viewed as completely interior– all in the mind, unpossessing of an external reality.

Such a division is ridiculous.

The human mind often seeks external causes– the seeking for both gods and scientific theory is born of the *same impulse.* This makes certain people uncomfortable.

It comes from a very visceral survival method– recognising patterns which are either detrimental or beneficial. This is an animal thing, pre-human and actually extraordinarily successful.

If it wasn't, you wouldn't be here.

It comes from pre-conscious times. It's innate, and inborn, part of our heredity. So, given that's true, what of the "second birth" of the spirit?

Suppose it's only a metaphor? Suppose one birth is actually all we need, that all the shifts in awareness suggested in myth are methods of returning to– a reacquisition of – faculties rendered latent by socialization– as we *unlearn* "reality" as it was handed to us?

What happens when a system breaks, when the precarious functioning of society is disrupted by cultural shift or natural disaster? We're witnessing it now, with the insurrections across the Middle-East and the situation in Japan.

The myriad narratives spinning into existence, the hysteria and sense of foreboding – the sense that things are rushing headlong out of control, and the desperate attempt to try and make sense of things– all these are triggering, or are effects of our latent survival instinct.

Obviously a robust system is desirable– something that can endure such events. Most of the extremely clever people on the ground are already trying to alter things so that their systems don't fail next time.

Because that's a sensible thing to do. But sometimes, no matter how robust a system, an event will occur that breaks it. It may be of a tiny level of possibility, say once in a million years but it *will* occur, and it will come in a way which bypasses our control.

So what do we do, if even the most robust system may break?

What if we could build systems that weren't just robust, but are in fact *afragile*? What if you could make a thing that worked even *better* when it was at that breaking point? Accepting the rupture and utilizing it.

Evolution works on *afragile* principles to a point– the survival of the fit. Selection pressures mean that eventually an organism arrives which functions better in its environment than its predecessors.

There is an assumption that in disasters, people panic. Yet recent events have proved otherwise– *e.g.* the Japanese scuba-diving badass Hideaki Akaiwa who swims through a swamped city daily rescuing people.

This works for ancient events as well. Around 60,000 years ago, the whole of the human species was in Africa– down to just 2,000 of us. Humans were an endangered species and yet we prevailed because of social ties.

Oral storytelling and myth-making is an afragile practice, too. Don't believe me?– then look no further than the world of pro-wrestling– when fictionalized story-lines replaced the previously standard plays of "catch-wrestling," the industry began to evolve into a multi-billion dollar industry.

And when it became clear that much of wrestling was fictive– when the story-lines were deliberately designed to entice and entertain– rather than simple actuality, instead of signaling the death-knell for the sport, it allowed more intricate and engrossing plots via the practice known as *kayfabe*.

So what does this boil down to?

By accepting ourselves as native to the mythic– that it runs through our blood and physicality and has done so since the beginning of us, we no longer have to look *elsewhere* for the door to such spaces.

An *incunabulum* is an early printed pamphlet or book, with its Latin roots in 'swaddling clothes' and figurative childhood. As a natives of the mythic, we are living texts, incarnate in gonzo-bodies.

We are all incunabula. We are changelings already.

All the mythic properties ascribed to the external are products of interpretations of physical stimuli. In order to find their source we simply must unlearn our ideas of what is possible.

We cannot escape our physicality, our senses– the notion of an "out there" will never actually be made manifest in us. We must unlearn "reality," itself.

Incunabula II:

Cut ups and Becoming

Mr. VI

When you cut into the present the future leaks out.

William S. Burroughs.

Previously, I've spoken of the incunabula– natives of the mythic. I've argued that the distinction between between myth and reality is meaningless because "reality" as we know it is a model, a narrative created to comprehend our perceptions; reality as we know it is born out of the same construction process that we use to make myth and spin our tales.

You can't separate it from physicality, because the physical is our interface with the wider universe. It's as intimate as blood, breath and bone, as vital as sexual secretions and just as rich.

And just like those fluids, it's a lubricant; a fluid-smooth space that allows flow and transverse movement. It contains the potential for life, and also death and disease of the psyche.

It's not a thing of top-down authority and hierarchy, indeed if there is any movement which could be described as solely vertical in terms of myth, it's an *upwelling*– born from the ground of being itself– bottom up. If divinity presents itself to us at all, it is up from the dirt not down from the heavens.

Urðarbrunnr. The Well of Wyrd; the dwelling place of the Weird Sisters, the *Nornir* who lay down and weave the events of a person's life into what they will become.

Cut, arrange, and put together; folding events in and under over. Perhaps Burroughs was more right than he knew, perhaps it's not the *future* that leaks out when you cut the present, but the wyrd-fluid, the raw material for *becoming?*

Make the incision, cut the flesh and the vital fluid wells up– for incunabula the blood of their body flows free, an opening is made to serve as entrance and exit. It becomes an access port to their own *becoming-as...*

Endorphins get you high, get you soaring, get you awake and alive. Opening yourself, creating a gate to the unknown, the unintelligible spaces beyond the senses. It's blood magic, to feed and gift yourself to all comers.

We'll come back to that later– for now recall that the body-as-text is an essential of the incunabula. That being the case, who owns the text? Who has the right to edit and re-write its narrative?

Glossy magazines and moral prohibitions; eidolons of form to aspire to– these are not bottom-up processes. No, they are hierarchical and top-down. The individual must operate as a thrall to such imagery– authorative texts.

Taxonomy via text– classification and definition; truly People of the Book, an inviolate and holy manuscript.

An immovable arrangement of form, sanctified by divinity because YHVH made humanity in his own image and there's only one divinity, yes?

The brimming cornucopia of myth says otherwise; this apparent transcendent authority is not alone. *Kami, landvaettir, alfar, dwergar* and *muses. Annunaki, shedim* and *lilitu, bodhisattvas, asuras* and *daevas. Nagas, tulpas, piskies, puccas* and *ghul.*

Not one text– and the knowledge of this is reaching common awareness now– for did G-d have a wife? Anyone with half an interest will smile and tell you this is nothing new. Asherah has been around for years, god-wife or no.

But the incunabula makes the ink into blood, running on skin, carving out new juxtapositional language by dismembering the old, powerful creation. Just ask Odin, Marduk or any personages– human or not– who've broken things down, remixed them and come up with something new.

There's a glorious multiplicity of form here; the fluid spaces of becoming certainly echoing the amniotic fluid.

The poem by Gabe Moses entitled "How to Make Love to a Trans Person" speaks loudly of such wonderful becomings and though it's a little long to reproduce, here's an excerpt:

> Forget the images you've learned to attach
>
> To words like cock and clit,
>
> Chest and breasts.
>
> Break those words open
>
> Like a paramedic cracking ribs
>
> To pump blood through a failing heart.
>
> Push your hands inside.
>
> Get them messy.
>
> Scratch new definitions on the bones.
>
> Get rid of the old words altogether.

The incunabula must know that they are their own authority on themselves. The awareness of this lends them a kind of strange– some might say spiritual– strength that enables them to operate outside of notions of property or category.

Others may attempt to shape them, contour them, but they are covered in that new fluid which comes from within them, pulsing with every heartbeat. Nothing sticks– it is carried away on a tide of metaphor, ever unreachable.

For they understand something– that we are creatures of language, that our cognition is intimately bound up with our bodies. Don't believe me? Then answer me how getting up high increasing charitable donations, why don't you?

We've all felt it; the freezing stare, the cold shoulder, the burning lust.

So what about diving down, to plunge into the depths inside us?

Piercing, scarification, tattooing, all these can be simple things, or they can be ways of bringing visions into flesh, incarnating and grounding them in the intimate processes of existence. Just as sex can be a perfunctory release of tension, or can be an almost mystic communion, so can all bodily functions– the performance sanctified by millions of years of successful ancestors.

And if the universe ends beyond the reaches of our senses as far as direct carnal knowledge goes, then who knows what lies beyond those boundaries; more to the point, what lies *within* us, beneath our conscious awareness?

What comes to call at the presence of the fluidic becomings, the plasmic offerings of potential? What seats itself about us and consumes the food offered on the altars of our bodies?

If the flesh is so central to humanity, then we must necessarily acknowledge its decay, its movements and metabolism, its sags and wrinkles, ripples and self-combustions. To do otherwise is to create an escapist narrative that ultimately ends in exhaustion and failure.

Each chapter is a bounded slice of experience, each word an embodied thought, but their arrangement is limitless. Death may not be an end, but instead an integral experience which informs the rest of the narrative. Burroughs speaks again:

The cut-up is actually closer to the facts of perception than representational painting. Take a walk down a city street and put down what you have just seen on canvas. You have seen a person cut in two by a car, bits and pieces of street signs and advertisements, reflections from shop windows– a montage of fragments. Writing is still confined to the representational straitjacket of the novel ... consciousness is a cut up. Every time you walk down the street or look out of the window, your stream of consciousness is cut by random factors.

Resolutions

James Curcio

Yesterday morning, I finished reading Murakami's *Norwegian Wood*.

It was raining, unusually cold for an August morning, and almost coal black. I couldn't imagine a better morning to finish this particular book. I sat in silence for a good hour after closing the cover, thinking to myself. (Who else would I think to?) Beethoven was playing in the background. It colored all my thoughts for the rest of the day.

While reading, I suggested it to several people, and one of them asked me if I could explain the ending to her. She was looking for a sort of resolution that Murakami seems typically reticent to provide.

As a result, I've been thinking about resolutions. Well, I've been thinking about many things, but one of the threads is resolution. I'll share my notes, and hope that you aren't offended by "spoilers," because personally, I could give a damn– any story worth reading is worth reading.

The idea of "spoilers" themselves gives us a starting point. There are certain expectations that most readers put on *endings*. They want everything wrapped up and explained for them, as if the purpose of every narrative is to create a series of questions and then answer them all with a declarative, final conclusion. It's an unrealistic expectation, given the nature of life– often the endings that count the most seem to come unexpectedly, out of nowhere. You're crossing the road thinking about the complications posed by the two women you love, and wham! a truck hits you. That's it. These endings resolve nothing, but they're brutally honest.

Some of us want certain types of the fantastical in our literature for many reasons and that's one of them. But there are no necessities here, and if one thing has been done a thousand times, why not explore another?

My point is, endings and resolutions are not the same, and an ending doesn't need to resolve anything. Something can end, people can drop out of our lives as if they had instead dropped off the face of a steep cliff, but there is no resolution. Similarly something can resolve, and in the process transform into something else, which is a way whereby an end can be turned into a beginning. The Death card in the Tarot is said to be a resolution, for instance. It isn't necessarily an ending.

Finally, resolutions are something that we *set ourselves toward*. That seems very different at first, but the goals on our horizon, and the ends we meet aren't necessarily that far off from one another, sometimes.

Now that we've got that straight, I'd like to return to Murakami's ending for *Norwegian Wood*, and its lack of resolution.

I phoned Midori.

"I have to talk to you," I said. "I have a million things to talk to you about.

A million things we have to talk about. All I want in this world is you. I want to see you and talk. I want the two of us to begin everything from the beginning."

Midori responded with a long, long silence— the silence of all the misty rain in the world falling on all the new-mown lawns of the world. Forehead pressed against the glass, I shut my eyes and waited.

At last, Midori's quiet voice broke the silence: "Where are you now?"

Where was I now? Gripping the receiver, I raised my head and turned to see what lay beyond the phone box. Where was I now? I had no idea. No idea at all. Where was this place? All that flashed into my eyes were the countless shapes of people walking by to nowhere. Again and again I called out for Midori from the dead centre of this place that was no place.

Here the protagonist is calling Midori— the girl he has decided he wants to be with after the suicide of his first lover, Naiko— and she is distant, but she does take his call, which reaches her as if over this great expanse. When I read it, it seemed as if the camera was pulling away at the end of a movie, and he's just this little piece of jetsam floating in the ocean. The protagonist fades into a sea of people, no longer central, no longer even notable. Just a face, a dot, nothing at all. More notable, you never find out what Midori's reply is. There is no resolution.

This seems to be a common element in Murakami's stories, for instance there is an intentional suspension of resolution in many short stories in *The Elephant Vanishes*, and it is a tendency that I personally find refreshing, given how much pressure I've been handed as an author to always resolve everything. Tying threads together, as if, should we leave some hanging, they will come lose in our minds, and the whole story might unravel. When you don't, some people accuse you of bad or sloppy plot-work, as if you simply forgot to resolve that which you intentionally left unresolved.

Another misconception that arises from this approach is that it is at all new. It has been one way of ending a piece of classical music since Beethoven, radical that he was, played games with the form. There is an echo of the Enlightenment project in this approach that appeals to our sense of harmony and symmetry, everything in its place, every element a counterpoint to another, all tensions built and resolved.

This tension creation and resolution process is identical to what we find in music. One example of many: though no stranger to the use of the dissonant "devil's interval," (minor 3rd) Bach was a master at overwhelming us with harmony. Beethoven presented more of the Romantic sentiment. He was, strange as it may seem to us now, in many ways a rebel. At the end of some Beethoven pieces, he ends on an unresolved chord.

Murakami is employing the same kind of ending. Our underlying aesthetic, cultural, and philosophical presuppositions structure our composition of fiction. If it is not done intentionally, it occurs all on its own. What does it say about our view of the world that we compose– or consume– stories that are one way and not another? What we don't say gives away more than what we do. The closing fragment of *Norwegian Wood* echoes in a void, much like that repeated chord at the end of the Moonlight Sonata, reaching out for something that can't be touched.

Lack of resolution makes us uneasy. Maybe it reflects or amplifies the fear of our own lack of resolution. But it also provokes a sense of being haunted. The story lives on as a shadow, a relationship ended without closure. That's how I felt as I sat there with the book closed in my lap, staring out into the rain and nothing in particular. Like Naiko's ghost, lingering in an unanswered reply.

We shouldn't feel pressure to resolve our stories in any particular way. Our job is to find what a story wants to be and help nurture it. Some pieces may call for a classic resolution, or even a twist on your repeated theme, like the cliché at the end of a blues tune, a coda where the impression seems almost an ironic telegraph– "here is the ending you were expecting, ok? Go home."

But if the resolution to a story would require a new book, then maybe give your reader a wall of mist, rather than that. You aren't law-bound to provide a resolution as your ending. Midori's answer, given across that immense expanse, is the beginning of a new story, not the ending of that one.

Not all calls are answered. Not all chords are resolved.

Contesting "Human Nature"

The Psychology of Power

James Curcio

The Occupy Wall Street movement has taken aim at "the 1%," but so far there has not been a great deal of consideration given to the culture or psychology of power.

Countering the charged, idealistic cry of the protesters comes the more cynical stance that "there will always be a 1%." That, perhaps, it is human nature to claw our way to the "top of the pile," to slay the sitting King and take the throne. Certainly, that is a model we see mirrored in the heroic myths of antiquity.

As a result of our nature, are we forever cursed to live out a narrative of master / slave, of fascist dictator, of oppressor and oppressed? Should we resign ourselves to the "grim meathook future" that seems the inevitable outcome of the myth of the Leviathan, supposing no agents of chaos destabilize the everpresent obsession of fascism? Not control as an end in itself, but rather control as the means to order and homogenization. This is the true face of the New American Century: one of peace secured through violence, possibly tooled atop a myth of racial purity.

The "natural" claim of power is the first that should be considered. There is no absolutely solid, demonstrable proof that the inclination to power is a natural human instinct rather than a culturally re-enforced or selected one, or that power "always" corrupts. There is a high burden of proof for such claims, and investigation of such questions tends more towards myth-making than the method of science.

Nevertheless, the stance of an inherent "will to power" seems to be supported by Neitzsche's stance, that even survival is of lesser concern to animals than the will to power. Due to his aphoristic style it is particularly easy to misrepresent Nietzsche's position on anything, but it is possible his love of the heroic myths that do center on the will to power, versus the "slave" mythos of Christianity, makes the role of the will to power seem like a force of nature.

In one way or another, many still uphold myths about human nature and the nature of political power that have their origin in treatises many hundreds of years old. Let's look at some of these myths, even if only in passing, and consider what we can know, and what is merely cruel conjecture, beginning with research mentioned in a recent Alternet article looking at todays plutocrats:

The first revelation came from Dr. Nassir Ghaemi of Tufts University. In his recent book, "A First-Rate Madness," he went beyond merely restating the old adage that anyone crazy enough to run for public office probably shouldn't occupy that office. Instead, the book sheds light on what Ghaemi calls an "inverse law of sanity," whereby tumultuous times like these actually reward and promote political figures who are "mentally abnormal (or) even ill."

Now comes a new study from Switzerland's University of St. Gallen showing that the most successful of the global financial elite probably pose more of a menace to society than known psychopaths.

To summarize, the problem isn't necessarily that power "always corrupts," as it could be equally true that those obsessed enough with power to pursue it with the kind of monomaniacal fixation required to succeed may also be thereby artificially "selected" to otherwise be *fucking bonkers.* A causes B; B causes A.

Though, as with most mammals I'm aware of, there are clearly some innate power structures hard-wired I've yet to see any clear proof that a pyramid model of power is innate to our nature. There's been some argument made by an array of primatologists and anthropologists that we have conflicting impulses in regard to cooperation and competition, and to our aid in creating an easy to grasp dialectic, the bonobo gallantry struts into the picture, as contrasted with the more violent chimpanzee. (And then promptly gets distracted by the lure of group sex and honey on a reed straw.)

The origin of human aggression and warfare remains hotly debated. Until now, this debate has been dominated by what chimpanzees do and how this compares with our own species. It is little known, however, that we have an exactly equally close primate relative, the bonobo. This species makes Hobbesians very uncomfortable, so they do everything to marginalize it. One anthropologist seriously suggested that we should ignore bonobos, because they are close to extinction, not realizing that by the same token we should also ignore "Lucy," "Ardi" and all those other ancestors that bit the dust. Others treat bonobos as a wonderful afterthought, a great curiosity, but irrelevant to where we come from. **Scientific American, Waal.**

The point is that "us" / "them" mentality and tribalism is certainly a part of our makeup, but it's a bit like the wild conjecture of Hobbes or Rousseau to take that several steps further and make claims about what that singular "human nature" is.

Rousseau criticized Hobbes for asserting that since man in the "state of nature . . . has no idea of goodness he must be naturally wicked; that he is vicious because he does not know virtue." On the contrary, Rousseau holds that "uncorrupted morals" prevail in the "state of nature" and he especially praised the admirable moderation of the Caribbeans in expressing the sexual urge. **Discourse on Inequality, Rousseau.**

To summarize, Hobbes felt that it was the purpose of a controlling state to protect man from himself, whereas Rousseau saw the state itself as the source of "evil."

Let's try to take a less polarizing view. What is our reason to believe that there is a *singular* nature innate in us in regard to power? Clearly, "human nature" is a myth, but what is its agenda?

Regardless of how we are raised or who we are, the truism goes, "absolute power corrupts absolutely." I would propose that instead of a singular, innate "will to power," it is more likely that, as with genes, we have many possibilities provided but only several which are activated by chance and circumstance. It shouldn't have required Harry Harlowe's "Pit of Despair" to demonstrate that a key difference between feral, abusive primates and nurturing, loving ones resides in the treatment they themselves received. Primates will often choose affection or even the illusion of it from a soft surrogate stuffed "mother" than food itself. (The history that goes in the books– genocide, torture, war– is this the history of child abuse?)

I'd still stick to my claim that the appearance of the psychology of power is actually the psychology of a particular "type" (or several) which are most prone to *take* power. Then consideration of power becomes a study on the ideology of fascism, not human nature at large. We can look outward at the social structures that support the growth of the fascistic tendency in our own nature, the tendencies against which we should be vigilant if we don't want to live under the yoke of such restriction. These types are greatly supported not only by our own culture, but also by the vast majority of state-cultures in recorded history. It is not merely a Western phenomenon, for surely we can look to the history of ancient China or Japan and see the will to power manifesting itself in a totalitarian manner. The will to power is certainly not a provincial cultural peculiarity.

Regardless, we don't need to be co-opted by the myths that support this power structure. We can begin within the "one square foot of real estate" of our own mind. However, as Jefferson said, "the price of eternal freedom is vigilance." Resisting and restructuring such power structures is not at all easy. Power has an annoying habit of turning us into hosts for its demands.

In regard to a republic, the best leaders would be those who are not entirely excited about the idea of being in such a position. Those whose every impulse is to lead by force (psychological or otherwise) should probably be kept far away from political office. (Put them in charge of MMORGs or something.) It seems to me that Greek philosophy arose, among other things, hand-in-hand with the demands of their democratic system. If you're going to try to take the floor, you'd best learn rhetoric.

Our shared history seems to support the premise that the end result of any over-reaching state is either collapse, domination by another state, or totalitarianism. This is the "result" we judge the human will to power from.

But– to dodge what would otherwise easily become a long dissertation on world history that I'm ill-equipped to provide– we are missing the full picture if we make an evaluation based only from results, even if they have been repeated time and again. The results that seem to imply a "human nature" of power and dominance are enmeshed in a *matrix of circumstance, opportunity, and evolutionary selection processes that favor certain dispositions.* It's not a given, it's not "nature"– as a fundamental change of the social mechanisms themselves would change that "nature." e.g. It isn't *innate* in an intrinsic sense, even if the propensity for such behavior clearly exists in our biology.

To support this, we can refer back to that Alternet article,

> *Obviously, these results reflect the not-so-surprising fact that the extreme nature of the modern political process and of today's casino economy inherently self-select for certain kinds of traits.*

> *As the website Newser reported, the researchers "pitted a group of stockbrokers against a group of actual psychopaths in various computer simulations and intelligence tests and found that the money men were significantly more reckless, competitive, and manipulative." Even more striking, the researchers note that achieving overall success was less important to the stock speculators than the sadistic drive "to damage their opponents."*

Again, these selection processes (or the end result of them) can make it *seem* that "humans in power are always X way," but what we're seeing is a systemic effect, not a purely innate one. So, the salient question then becomes whether we can create sustainable social and economic systems that self-select for the traits that we actually *want* in our leaders and fellow citizens.

That is the question that we need to be asking. It is the model that we need to build our social mechanisms from, or else we will be doomed to repeat the same pattern time and again, and it won't matter a bit if its source is innate or conditioned. There is possibly nothing more crucial to our development or even survival in the next century than this.

Nuclear Power in the Kali Yuga

David Metcalfe

...The fact of the release of nuclear energy, overwhelming and intoxicating though it was, began to seem less tremendous. Was it not simply the first act, even a mere prelude, in a series of fantastic events which, having afforded us access to the heart of the atom, would lead us on to overthrow, one by one, the many other strongholds which science is already besieging? The vitalization of matter by the creation of super-molecules. The re-modeling of the human organism by means of hormones. Control of heredity and sex by the manipulation of genes and chromosomes. The readjustment and internal liberation of our souls by direct action upon springs gradually brought to light by psycho-analysis. The arousing and harnessing of the unfathomable intellectual and effective powers still latent in the human mass. . . . Is not every kind of effect produced by a suitable arrangement of matter? And have we not reason to hope that in the end we shall be able to arrange every kind of matter, following the results we have obtained in the nuclear field? **Some Reflections on the Spiritual Repercussions of the Atom Bomb, Pierre Teilhard De Chardin**

Having been well cured in the after glow of the first nuclear tests at Trinity, it's rare today to find those who fully appreciate the weight of those discoveries. In Teilhard De Chardin's analysis, written in 1946 shortly after the terrible events at Hiroshima and Nagasaki, Humanity has discovered a sure sign of its unlimited potential. Rather than an end point, he sees the atomic bomb as just the beginning of a new stage of evolution in which Humanity is crowned with the glory of knowledge and comes full face with the roots of existence.

We know today that this discovery is not so easily contained, and the myth of atomic power has a much darker protagonist than the glowing god of progress that was first envisioned. Each of the categories that he discusses are attended by an endless stream of seemingly insurmountable ethical questions within the present state of society. The science of genetics is in the hands of corporations, pharmaceutical companies and a limping Academy, the issues that surround disposal of nuclear waste have stopped development of any far reaching use of nuclear power, and the reactors that have been built are currently decaying under a lapsed economy that cannot support heavy infrastructure maintenance.

The dangers of our ignorance have most recently been shown in the ongoing tragedy of the reactor meltdowns occurring in Japan. We face an aging population of scientists who have the skills and knowledge that have maintained these reactors up to this point. The physicists, metallurgists and chemists who designed, built and maintain these sites are getting older, or have already passed on, and due to the focus of the Academy on providing 'thought leaders' and technicians who are ready to 'face the future,' we have left behind much of the knowledge necessary to keep up with what we have.

Some foresaw the tragic potential in this exploration of the inner sanctum of Nature. Writing in the 1950's the anonymous alchemist Fulcanelli discusses a less democratically optimistic view of these advances:

> *God the Father holds in his hand this globe, surmounted by the fiery sign. The four great ages– historical representations of the four ages of the world– have their sovereigns shown holding this same attribute. They are Alexander, Augustus, Charlemagne and Louis XIV.3 It is this which explains the inscription INRI, exoterically translated as Iesus Nazarenus Rex Iudeorum (Jesus of Nazaredi, King of the Jews), but which gives to the cross its secret meaning: Igne Nalura Renovatur Integra (By fire nature is renewed whole). For it is by fire and in fire that our hemisphere will soon be tried. And just as, by means of fire, gold is separated from impure metals, so, Scripture says, the good will be separated from the wicked on the great Day of Judgment.*

> *The first three are emperors, the fourth is only a king, the Sun King, thus indicating the decline of the star and its last radiation. This is dusk, the forerunner of the long cyclic night, full of horror and terror, "the abomination of desolation.* **Mystery of the Cathedrals, Fulcanelli**

In alchemical terms this discovery was not the achievement of the Great Work, but the discovery of just one more False Light held up as a distraction and trap. Rather than find the Secret Fire which is attendant to the perfection of the Philosopher's Stone, they merely encapsulated and unleashed the deadly potential of the Central Fire, whose positive symbolic form is the Fire of Life and thus in polarity the Fire of Death. Following the traditional philosophy of cyclical movement, Fulcanelli foresaw this exemplary act of hubris in the form of technological advances that outpace the moral, intellectual and spiritual advances necessary to maintain them.

> *In Hindu mythology, the four equal sectors of the circle, formed by the cross, were the basis of a rather strange mystical conception. The entire cycle of human evolution is figured there in the form of a cow, symbolizing Virtue, each of whose four feet rests on one of the sectors representing the four ages of the world.*

In the first age, corresponding to the Greek age of gold and called the Creda Yuga or age of innocence, Virtue is firmly established on earth: the cow stands squarely on four legs. In the Treda Yuga or second age, corresponding to the age of silver, it is weakened and stands only on three legs. During the Touvabara Yuga, or third age, which is the age of bronze, it is reduced to two legs. Finally, in the age of iron, our own age, the cyclic cow or human virtue reaches the utmost degree of feebleness and senility: it is scarcely able to stand, balancing on only one leg. It is the fourth and last age, the Kali Yuga, the age of misery, misfortune and decrepitude. The age of iron has no other seal than that of Death. Its hieroglyph is the skeleton, bearing the attributes of Saturn: the empty hourglass, symbol of time run out, and the scythe, reproduced in the figure seven, which is the number of transformation, of destruction, of annihilation. The Gospel of this fatal age is the one written under the inspiration of St. Matthew. Matthaeus, Greek Ματθαῖος, comes from Ματταθίας, which means science. This word has given μελέτη, μνημονικός, study, knowledge, from μάθετε, to learn. It is the Gospel according to Science, the last of all but for us the first, because it teaches us that, save for a small number of the elite, we must all perish. For this reason the angel was made the attribute of St. Matthew, because science, which alone is capable of penetrating the mystery of things, of beings and their destiny, can give man wings to raise him to knowledge of the highest truths and finally to God. **Mysteries of the Cathedrals, Fulcanelli**

There is a Loretta Lynn song titled "Everyone wants to go to Heaven, but nobody wants to die," that speaks very plainly to the issue at hand. Every one wants the advances of technology, but too many lack the humility, the ego transformed in death, to truly benefit. Worse, those who are actively pursuing development in these areas have proven time and again that their quest is based on idle curiosity, vainglory or envy.

I spoke of the Spirit of the Earth. What are we to understand by that ambiguous phrase?

Is it the Promethean or Faustian spirit: the spirit of autonomy and solitude; Man with his own strength and for his own sake opposing a blind and hostile Universe; the rise of consciousness concluding in an act of possession?

Is it the Christian spirit, on the contrary: the spirit of service and of giving; Man struggling like Jacob to conquer and attain a supreme center of consciousness which calls to him; the evolution of the earth ending in an act of union?

Spirit of force or spirit of love? Where shall we place true heroism, where look for true greatness, where recognize objective truth?

It would take too long, and it is outside the scope of this paper, to discuss the comparative worth of two opposed forms of adoration, the first of which may well have attracted poets, but only the second of which, I think, presents itself to the reflective mind as capable of conferring upon a universe in motion its full spiritual coherence, its total substance beyond death, and finally its whole message for our hearts.(Witnesses of that experiment in Arizona found, in the anguish of the last instants, that in the depths of their hearts they were praying. [Official Report: appendices.])

What does matter here is to note that Mankind cannot go much further along the road upon which it has embarked through its latest conquests without having to settle (or be divided intellectually on) the question of which summit it must seek to attain.

In short, the final effect of the light cast by the atomic fire into the spiritual depths of the earth is to illumine within them the over-riding question of the ultimate end of Evolution– that is to say, the problem of God. **Some Reflections on the Spiritual Repercussions of the Atom Bomb, Pierre Teilhard De Chardin**

Both Teilhard De Chardin and Fulcanelli saw the end point of these advances to be a meeting with the Divine, with the end point of Being. What Fulcanelli has pointed out with more honesty is that such a meeting is always attended by a trial, and that the quest for Illumination requires a sacrifice. Despite the title of his Reflections leading one to think that they explore the spiritual repercussions of the atomic bomb, Teilhard De Chardin's analysis remains firmly rooted in the physical sphere, blind to the full implication of *Igne Natura Renovatur Integra* "By fire nature is renewed whole," and lacking the realization that Actaeon, upon his vision of Diana, was devoured by his own dogs.

Postmodernogamy, Polyamory,

and the Marriage Narrative

James Curcio

Postmodernogamy is a playful perversion of language, a facetious neologism that I've been using for several years.

Let me explain it to you in my usual round-about way.

A conversation sparked up with Rowan, (whose pieces you recently read), off of his use at one point of the term "Postmonogamy," which is of course different from "postmodernogamy" altogether.

I was only half awake when I read it, so I somehow assumed that he had said "postmodernogamy." The ensuing conversation went somewhere both insightful and absurd, doubly so now that I realize it was all based on a misunderstanding on my part. (I, in fact, have very little to contribute to the idea of postmonogamy. I think it's unnecessary, and I'm sure we'll have a faux debate about that any day now.)

So, though it is the result of a minor misunderstanding before I had my morning coffee, something interesting occurred. *Felix Culpa*. I'd like to share my thoughts with you on the transition of relationships from the archaic to modern to postmodern age. Tongue-in-cheek, yes. But not toothless. Hopefully I needn't spell the general narrative of that obvious mythically implied linearity. It was the stuff of most of our education, formal and otherwise. De Sade foretold the death of the social convention of marriage, a "slap in the face to the Apollonian man."

De Sade was, arguably, shaking his cage bars and fighting the formality of his time in the only ways he knew how. But there does seem to be a hysteria evident throughout much of the populace today, evidenced by the conflicts over gay marriage, and the fore-coming arguments about progressive group marriage (as opposed to regressive forms as seen for example in Mormonism) that are only beginning to hit the News.

The argument goes that marriage is meant to be between a man and a woman, and should this be contested, should it be sufficiently compromised, the entire fabric of society will collapse. We will revert to man-apes. Jesus will rise from the dead (again?!) and unleash his zombie hoards. Horrific stuff. Unless you like zombies, which apparently some people do.

If our society hangs from such a fragile thread, if we're dangling so precipitously from the edge of the cliff, then it seems inevitable that we will slide to the bottom. I say we do it champagne glasses in hand. But let's back up a moment. Isn't it plainly apparent that marriage has nothing to do with biology? My wife and I kissed (and etc) with several wonderful ladies at our wedding after-party, and I've yet to see a single zombie. (Though we should really get married more often, it seems to produce excellent parties.)

The restrictions applied to marriage, or applied through marriage, are representative of culturally normalizing forces within the society itself. They do not represent some kind of natural, let alone categorical, imperative. Though, of course, the pair bonding of mammals for the purpose of procreation does represent a biological imperative and I'll get to that in a moment.

To begin, I propose that our sexuality is not something that should structure our relationships, any more than our gender should restrict our behavior. Certainly not with such totality.

I don't say any of this as some kind of opponent of monogamy. My contention is with the *de facto expectation* that it is enforced as the norm in all cases, and I have a reservation about the hierarchy formed in modern life: rampant promiscuity when "dating" and "free" to either an ongoing string of serial monogamous relationships, or "settling down" which also implies "shutting out." In plain language, people are flaky as hell and fuck like rabbits when they're single and dating, and boring as fuck when they're not. I've lost more friends, at least practically speaking, to marriage than cancer or any other disease. I would not like to confine myself to this strict narrative.

Postmodernogamy is no solution. It is an orientation, and an acknowledgment that with being opened to more love, one is also opened to more pain. Nothing is easy, nothing always works. Life and relationships are not something that requires a constant solution, because they can't have one. They are bound to fall apart. The choice to face that inevitability with the full opposition of love is a radical act, a Luciferian act defying nature itself. That is true regardless of if we orient ourselves monogamously or polyamorously, much as a monotheist or polytheist have more in common with one another than with an atheist.

What are the alternatives, and what the hell does this have to do with postmodernism? Often the accusation leveled at bisexuality and polyamory alike, when other options are expended, is that it is *selfish*. This accusation is meant to immediately carry a negative connotation, I imagine, thanks to Abrahamic morality. (Which so often uses piety to mask various forms of selfishness, but that's another thing.) How many orgasms do you deserve? *Deserve*? Is it unhealthy? Are your hands going to sprout hair? No. That's as nonsensical an idea as someone dying for your sins.

Though any relationship that endures can't be based entirely on selfishness, I still have to question the underlying logic being employed here. What does it mean to be selfish in these cases?

There was a speech given by a Canadian author and playwright Robert Davies called "The Virtue of Selfishness." It was directed at the graduating class of a specialized school who were all going into social work. He asked, in a nutshell, "How can you help others if you cannot help yourself?" (Ayn Rand also had some things to say about the virtues of selfishness but I don't like her politics so I'm biased.)

If we shut ourselves down or make ourselves in the image of what our partner wants us to be, strictly, then we can't be of any service to them. I have often seen a pattern in the most claustrophobic relationships that partners fall for something in someone, and then suffocate it and find themselves dissatisfied with the person they helped engineer. The demands we make on our lovers when we need them to be our "one and only" approaches a sort of narcissitic fascism if left unbridled. Sex is one of many possible channels in which we can relate to others. It can also be one of many implicit conditions under which we come together– let's be honest– but there's something despicable about rendering the sum-total of a human being to their genitals. Of course, the aesthetics of our sexuality may dictate it within the context of sex, but is that the only lens through which we can view others? Are we to consider others strictly from the perspective of how we can use them, or conversely, supplicate ourselves to their needs?

I'm not talking about compromise here, which is an essential part of any relationship. As always it is easy to paint abstract pictures in absolutes when reality tends to fall somewhere in-between.

There isn't, on the flip side, an inherent virtue in selfishness, either. Without any regard for anyone else, the only alliances we can forge are along the axis of very temporary mutual best interests. However, in less extreme cases, if we're being honest, it is the maintenance of mutual best interest that any relationship is maintained. Without that it coasts on inertia only until such a time that a stronger gravitational force, so to speak, pulls it to a new course.

Finally, I can get to my actual point:

Based on the ideology of those that oppose gay as well as open marriage, the ends towards which marriage are directed are progeny and the maintenance of a certain social order. These are the biological imperatives I spoke of conjoined with a set of social rules and expectations which, though they vary by place and time in some ways– for instance arranged marriages are no longer the norm in the Western world–they tend towards a fairly similar pattern, with the exception of cultural outliers. (Such as matriarchal Native American tribes, and so on.)

So the archaic and modernist marriage is born, which implies teleology as the establishment of progeny as successors is a movement towards an end, one's own end, and in terms of time as well a stratification of life is implied. Our purpose is defined by society, and a woman's body is merely the vessel through which progeny– may they be males!–are created for the sake of that societies growth and dominance.

Let's look at the pattern. It begins with birth, childhood and play, then young adulthood: experimentation and social training, college and breaking off from parents, the period of dating which is a code word in many cases for casual sex and genetic sorting (finding a suitable mate). We then have marriage, and a shift of emphasis, on creating a platform for the life that is to come. Then, finally, there comes the long period of toil until the "golden" period when the young have left the nest and the now-elderly can reflect before death.

This pattern changes slightly by society but it is ingrained by various mythologies and seems mostly constant world-wide. It is re-enforced by the myths, by the laws, and by the possible prosecution of the rest of society, should anyone contest the "God given" order of things. Women are still stoned to death for not falling lock-step in accord with the laws of terrified men with tiny penises.

The "end of history" that hearkened postmodernism is easily reflected in a skeptical attitude towards these patterns; hierarchical methods of time and behavior categorization are replaced with more fluid nonlinear approaches. The jumble can remain a jumble, chaos is striated through its own self organizing principles, and our task becomes simply being wherever we are, recognizing, responding, seeking to be aware– sometimes to suffer and fail miserably but also, we hope, fearlessly– rather than trying to organize the process of our lives through an imposed order that comes from without. Life is a series of flows. There are hierarchies and orders, but they are self-structuring, and tend to collapse and reform on their own whims. To put it far less abstractly, we aren't the ones in control. We never were, we never will be. The conscious mind is a little air bubble in a giant block of jello.

This is what defines the post-modern condition, as well as skepticism towards meta-narratives, one of which could well be called the "sanctity of marriage." Yet, I don't contest its sanctity, in fact I'd like to see more of the sacred in all of our lives. Instead, let's demand postmodern skepticism towards the *teleology of our existence as birthing machines*, of beings that must always follow the same narrative, the same progression; that our futures must self-organize to the whims and dictates that come from without rather than within. This is a similar methodology that we've adopted for this project, abhorring the pre-fabrication of Enlightenment reason.

You know what? Now that I think of it, I hate the term postmodernism, too. Fuck. I've grown too postmodern for postmodernism. Well, some day I'll find a categorization I can live with.

Others to ourselves

Friendship and Expectation

James Curcio

Most of those we call "friend" can't bear the full weight of our honesty. The inverse is also likely true. You imagine you can hear the moorings creak and groan when you stray too close, even, to whatever personal truths are mutually, exclusively taboo.

I can be completely honest with you, of course, because you are anonymous. Even if I know you, I can't control whether you read this or not. That forces a form of anonymous relation even though in another context we may know one another. It is easiest to have honesty in an environment of anonymity, as I have often found through years of writing my most personal secrets for all to see online or in various books. Let's not pretend that honesty is not itself drawn in relation to falseness, but it is a statement I can make all alone, singularly owned, and it is not said with any expectation of the response.

But how is that taboo actually determined? It never is. It comes, instead, by way of expectation. This expectation has an internal dynamism. The expectation engine, fueled by imagination, rainbows, and the belief that if we lived our lives speaking our truth (we'd be delusional to think it is The Truth) we might find ourselves antagonized and then entirely alone.

I hope you can already see a really odd idea taking form here, and though it might be fuzzy yet, it still has sharp edges. Our relationships are based on a kind of personal fantasy. Beginning at a time before we even have memory, in earliest childhood, we begin building relations, behaviors, habits, ultimately, our conscious selves, based on the expectation of what is mutually desirable, or at the least, safe. Kosher. Of course, this is not the only model available to us. Some may engage with the counter-clockwise current of rebellion, and shoot instead for the personally desirable, or even mutually undesirable. Yet somehow the fact remains that all of that is based on a kind of mutual compromise of imagined boundaries and past experience rather than what is empirically known about the present.

Two things seem very interesting to me about this.

1) All these states are liminal, all based on expectation rather than certainty. It is a form of semi-intentional, mutual ignorance. If we were to test by trangression of those imagined barriers, it would already be too late to maintain a status quo. Either it is transgression or it isn't, and either way our perception of the relationship is transformed, whether in some small particular or in a blinding apocalypse that leaves only fragments behind.

2) This bounded world of implication, expectation, in the vernacular, "pussy-footing" can barely be called friendship. It's a convenient mutual illusion in stasis, only bending those rules when it has been challenged. (And, take notice: no one wants to stay friends long with someone who is constantly testing boundaries, either personal or of the relationship. In small doses it is radical and transformative, but applied constantly it is absolutely exhausting.)

This seems to make a mockery out of ourselves as well as our friends, committing us to all play roles based on an imagined reaction against a future shadow.

All of this is done, from the moment of birth and individuation, against the terror that beats behind our eyelids: I am forever all alone. Distinct and estranged from the environment, known and knowing only possible in a negative relation ("...not that, not that, not that..."). That was the cost of recursive self-consciousness. But must it damn us to play this timid, cruel game on one another?

This is not some kind of veiled message for one individual or another, "psst! our relationship is based on a fiction." Not at all. I've witnessed this in thousands of permutations throughout my life. Our relationships, and the ego that is structured as a result of them is, oddly enough, an empirical unknown.

I have had lovers who had to in an absolute and final way kill our relationship, because they had built a self in relation to their ongoing *expectation of my expectation* that they quite simply could not live with. They had to kill it, and there was only one clear way to do that. Of course, this decision was arrived at not by way of logic but emotion. Years of reflection have shown it to be true time and again. When we feel trapped in a relationship it is not so much a trap or cage (unless it literally is, but that's another thing entirely) as an internal discomfort at the self we have built for the other.

This isn't about who wronged who, it isn't even about agency, as to a certain extent, the more we commit to a relationship, the less we commit to our immediate agency anyhow, as the relation becomes more and more ones perceptual center. We all wrong one another sometimes. The best of us do it unintentionally; or maybe, it is in the intent? It's hard to say. (I mean that from the outside, hurt and offense is unipolar, but when you count intent, we may have meant nothing of the kind, or taken what we had to survive, or actively sought revenge, and these are three very different acts with the same shared or mutual dimension.)

That self, the one you build so that you can relate with them, is your cage. The other may have little to do with it at all, as we build it out of what we imagine others want us to be. (As I said, even if we rebelliously try to act against this and forge our own way, we're participating in a similar game, only superficially polarized. That is, supposing you don't become a true hermit.)

If you doubt this line of inquiry, I challenge you to gather the presence of mind to think outside the boxes created by your relations with others, and then speak your thoughts, feelings, and convictions with the utmost clarity and honesty you can muster. You won't need to be a total asshole to find that many of your supposedly nearest and dearest will very quickly come to think of you as a stranger, and yet others, maybe, only existing on the periphery of your life because your present fiction won't or can't engage them, might be able to engage with that honesty, or at the least, create a more mutually beneficial narrative.

Further, there may be some "friends" who actually love you enough to work through your truth and theirs, day by day, moment by moment, despite the fact that it is not constructed with their best interests in mind. If so, you are lucky. But you will only know them if you have the conviction to jettison all the rest, and risk being alone.

For my part, as time goes by, I have come to think that one is better alone than forced to be someone else's wind-up doll. However, I cannot bring myself to think that relation is impossible. On that, we each need to make a decision, and what is more difficult, live by it. The more we do that, the less we are understood by others. But that may be the real price of freedom.

The Big Score

James Curcio

The pupils dilate. The rush of *expectation* met and satisfied.

Everyone who's done coke knows this: the expectation of the rush is as potent as the dopamine hit itself. Maybe more.

In a Behaviorist universe, we've come to understand the world in terms of this simple mechanism: supply and demand. We've stripped ourselves down, re-purposed myths of spirit, turned ourselves into hungry machines. And we're machines driven by predictable needs, rewarded by chemical combinations.

I could be describing a junky scoring their next fix, or of the promise of seduction rewarded. I could be describing the satisfaction we receive when our virtual characters level up, or when we vanquish virtual enemies with our vorpal sword of badassness. (Some of us will even ostensibly sell our children for in-game currency). Hollywood has devised various formulas involving the offset of expectation and the big payoff: the protagonist "gets the girl," the "bad guys" are destroyed by the hero after a fierce struggle. What is the chemical formula of fear, of love, of mindless compliance?

Like most of the things I contemplate, this train of thought has a grounding in personal experience. I was waiting in line at the Pharmacy, anticipating the refill of my prescription of Oxycodone.

I have a legal and demonstrable need: pinched nerves in my back. The physical dependence that results makes you no less sick when your supply is suddenly cut, but our myths about drug addiction are still harmfully misplaced. I wouldn't kick over a fruit stand if my supply was to go suddenly, unexpectedly dry as the Colorado river. I'd just puke and be in more back pain. The fiver in Grandma's purse is safe.

The reward that washes over me when I know a prescription has been filled isn't nefarious; it's the comfortable knowledge that if I wake up with an icy pain running through my legs, I know I can take something that'll make it all a little more bearable.

These pills are a comforting presence, like the State. And like the State, they aren't nearly as benevolent as they at first seem.

Now that's a thought. Where do we draw the line between one kind of pain and another?

Like so many Americans, I have anxiety and depression because I've not had a regularly paying job in two years, and doctors want to prescribe me medications for that as well because they can't prescribe me an income. That's the bitch of it, isn't it? Our reduction of self to neurochemical automatons has some really questionable repercussions, especially when married with a pharmaceutical industry operating out of a profit motive. If a doctor acknowledges that being broke is making me depressed, then why would Prozac be the solution? Shouldn't they prescribe me a trust fund? Pathological depression is source-less. "I feel depressed all the time and I don't know why." When the cause is plain to see, it may just be a natural, if useless, response to a shitty situation.

I'm thinking all of this standing in line. I'd describe my surroundings to you, except that none of it is relevant or interesting. It was a Walgreens like any other Walgreens. We were all a bunch of people, like any other people. All the products on the shelves are identical. We are not, but pretend to be.

As my prescription was filled, as I took a pill, as I washed it down with a sugar-laden drink, it dawned on me that I'm not some kind of unique case. It reminded me of something I'd known before I'd been laid off, what was it? Oh, right. Thursday... pay day. Direct deposit in the account, the surrogate mother smiles benignly from above. I just have the opportunity to get a less ubiquitous angle on this common experience, because *we are all junkies by proxy.*

Junkies to the core. Junkies to things far more dangerous than opiates. As a society, we are hooked on our junk so deeply that we'll rape the planet, we will screw each other over, we will do absolutely anything possible to get our fix. It's best if we can outsource and offset the damage done, avoid having to stare the damage we've caused dead in the eye. But either way, you know. We've gotta score.

I know this may piss some of you off. Many of our addictions aren't just socially acceptable. They are socially mandated. Re-enforced and entrenched in our ideologies so deeply that we think any other possibility is downright crazy. Gasoline, cash, sex. We are insatiable, and our myths re-enforce our right to these things. How dare anyone imply otherwise? One kind of addiction is bad, the other good. The Television tells me so.

Corporations and our government counts on our addictions, even if they didn't create them. (Blame biology, if you like. We certainly are predisposed toward some things more than others. We make children's breakfast cereal sugary, not olive-flavored for a good reason.) Our needs and insecurities and fears are predictable, and predictability can be leveraged for profit. No sooner would it come out that a meteor was rocketing towards Earth that corporations would go to work figuring out how they could turn a profit.

Even if we get past our personal fear of death, the things we use to pacify ourselves are pretty comical. "I was going to revolt, but I got a dulce cinnamon latte instead." Above everything else, we're addicted to comfort and safety. So long as we can maintain a square foot of real-estate that seems safe and familiar, we'll overlook even the most egregious horrors. Scouring the planet of life, but so long as we have our latte, our pill, our paycheck– whatever it is– we'll stay the course. When Americans can't get a hamburger and a beer, *that's* when our government should fear us.

I get it, man. I'm a junky too. I can barely leave the house without needing to get a mocha, can't go more than a few days without missing my favorite shows. I see what's happening to the environment, see the stress fractures forming in the cornerstone of our society. Like anyone else I want to get laid and eat well. Like everyone else I want to feel secure. The status quo presented to us by myths like the inherent value of a 9-5 job is hard to resist. I don't think I can ever go back to seeing the world the same again, though. I'm just buying time, now. That's what some meds do, whether they're painkillers or psych meds– they buy you time to fix the underlying problem. (Or not.) I'm working on what I'm passionate about and praying that something presents itself. I've taken the first step: I'm a junky, and I'm *not* talking about the pills.

If you can't even acknowledge your addictions, well. Then you've *really* got a problem.

Self-Immolation and the Heart of Revolution

Awakening Out of the Dream

David Metcalfe

The heart of revolutionary faith, like any faith, is fire: ordinary material transformed into extraordinary form, quantities of warmth suddenly changing the quality of substance. If we do not know what fire is, we know what it does. It burns. It destroys life; but it also supports it as a sort of heat, light and– above all– fascination. **James Billington, Fire in the Minds of Men, Origins of the Revolutionary Faith**

In November, 1990 a man set himself on fire in front of the U.S. Capitol. The news reports from the time say that the reasons for the man's act were unknown, no riots were forthcoming. Last year the cultural shifts in Egypt, Yemen and Algeria proved a different outcome in light of similar self-immolation. As individuals express their anger, alienation and rejection in self willed conflagration it is igniting their communities into violent uprisings shaking the foundations of global culture.

Our media reports the bare essentials of the acts: lost job, police harassment, oppressive officials; editorials pontificate on the meaning, craft clumsy hagiographies of the individuals involved. The past month there have been reports of self immolation attempts stretching across North Africa, through the Middle East, Central Asia and into China; riots and revolutions erupting in the wake of these incendiary public sacrifices. More than the descriptions, the very flesh on fire is enough to break open the tension flowing through the lives of the worlds hopeful and disaffected.

It is necessary to seize the suitable moment... with the smallest spark a great fire can be ignited... **Sylvain Marechal, Voyages of Pythagoras**

As I'm writing this a young man sits in protest in a Palestinian Mosque, part of the March 15 Youth Coalition who set up tents in the Bethlehem municipality to demand a new Palestinian national council and a unified Palestine. He is threatening to set himself on fire if the Coalition's demands are not taken seriously. Unlike the young gunmen we have seen emerge in the United States, whose outward acts of inflamed anxiety cause communities to hold vigils and encourage greater controls, these self sacrificial immolations "change the quality of the substance," of the estrangement, isolation and abuse, to open up the opportunity for cultural change.

Fire is a fluid element, summoned with self sacrifice it rushes through communal streams of thought, transforming dormant discontent and revolutionary potential into active heat. Death comes on as a cold reminder, when someone opens fire in a crowded room the sacrifice opens the void of our own mortality. Invoking fire, invoking change in such an act of stunning self willed abrogation, calls to the very essence of action, of life, inseminating the communal psyche with a heaving need to move and react.

It's better to light a candle than curse the darkness.

Peter Benenson, founder of Amnesty International, at a Human Rights Day ceremony on 10th December 1961.

Two years after Beneson spoke Thích Quảng Đức was guided by two Buddhist monks into the street in front of the Cambodian embassy in South Vietnam. As he stood patiently, one of the monks placed a cushion on the ground, Duc sat down, drawing himself into the traditional lotus position he offered a prayer to Amitabha Buddha as the other attendant monk poured gasoline over him, and then he lit himself on fire. His austere immovability as the flames erupted around him proved his protest against the Diệm regime's treatment of Buddhists in South Vietnam.

During a vigil candles are held to remember the dead, when human beings themselves become candles we are called to remember the living and rethink the ineffable community that binds us together. In 2006 a member of the Chicago jazz and improvisational scene, Malachai Richter, set himself on fire in protest of U.S. military actions in the Middle East. In an explanatory note he posted online he says

Maybe some will be scared enough to wake from their walking dream state - am I therefore a martyr or terrorist? I would prefer to be thought of as a 'spiritual warrior'.

For all intents he was an ordinary man, who he describes in his self written obituary as:

A lover of literature, even more than music, he had always dreamed of being a writer. The handwritten manuscript of his 'fictional autobiography', titled "Farewell Tour" was under consideration by publishers. It had a general theme of shared universal aloneness, and was controversial for seeming to endorse suicide after the age of fifty. His favorite classic authors were Proust and Shakespeare.

The metaphor for his life was winning the lottery, but losing the ticket. In the end, the loneliness was overwhelming. He was deeply appreciative for everything that had been given to him, but acutely aware that the greater the present, the higher the price. He was a member of Mensa, and Alcoholics Anonymous since 1990. For him, sobriety was virtually getting a second chance at life. He practiced a personal and private spirituality, seeking to connect across the illusion that separates us from each other. Reportedly, his last words were 'rosebud... oops'... and the epitaph that he chose is "I dreamt that I was dreaming.

In the fire all of that changed, from a guy you might run into at a jazz set, into a signpost for society and a condemnation of our inability to embrace each other. He left a simple note near where he lit himself on fire, a reminder for when the flames died down. It was a brief commandment for the governing powers of the world in hopes that life would prevail through the pain: *"Thou shalt not kill."*

God and the

Problem of Certainty

James Curcio

There is little more problematic than a religious zealot that doesn't even seem to understand the function of symbol, let alone the scientific method. But there is a similar side to self-assured atheism that strikes me in all earnestness like proverbial fingernails down a chalkboard. (More like a rusty nail.)

This perspective, quite simply, believes that if the theistic premise is irrational, it must be false. They often seem to strike a social posture in regard to this, laughing and prodding at theists like a group of British Colonials laughing at the stupid natives.

Granted, this perspective seems less dangerous. There have been few atheist inquisitions.

But it is still based on misunderstanding heaped upon misunderstanding, so I'd like to try to clarify a position. I'm quite sure I'll make no friends in doing so, but I simply can't help myself.

Let's get to it. Disproving God with science makes as little sense as proving God with science. From the vantage point of logic, God is at best a philosophical postulate, but beyond that, and more importantly, it is a relationship or orientation which one either does or doesn't have. Relationship with imaginary friend or material one, it's still a relationship with psychological import if you are actually invested in that belief.

Saying what I just did in some places and times could get you killed. We still kill one another as a result of misread metaphors and petty differences. The tension between religion and science remains a bomb ticking in our classrooms– made of equal parts C-4 and stupidity– created by people that don't seem to understand the function of either religion or science. It comes out to be a bit like claiming a bulldozer is true and a grapefruit is not. Take technology out of the equation and we have, unsurprisingly, not evolved a whole lot in fifteen hundred years. (Put it in the equation, and we still haven't, but that's a different story.)

In other words, primate pack behavior has a funny way of sneaking into our own packs. We've yet to outgrow it. Biologically, it may take a half million years.

Religion is, if anything at all, the ground upon which an experience can occur. What is it that we interact with when we reach into the void? It is not an idea in the sense that ideas are static, dead things. An experience such as this is not something to be proven or disproven, even if anyone with a brain can easily understand that there is nothing in physics that would lead us to take the doctrine and dogma of monotheist religion literally.

Nevertheless, the divinity premise that we assume to run through all theism is simply the belief that there is an intelligence behind the universe. This is an unprovable postulate. There's nothing to be found. It is exceedingly difficult to prove intelligence even when life is involved. (Consider various related quandaries in AI, when we can only know intelligence through its effects. We need acts to consider a mind, but with those acts we can't prove its existence. Even the existence of intelligence itself could be a symptom of a deeper, embedded intelligence. Or it may not be. Such recursions are a symptom of the metaphysical contemplation of consciousness. Only go there if you like halls of mirrors.)

So, divinity is not even considered within the project of science. Nor need it be. Science isn't an all inclusive method for rendering meaning out of personal experience. That is, of course, the role of myth. Nor would there be any point in faith if there was a need to "prove" God. It's a matter of apples and oranges.

But from this standpoint, proselytizing is inherently irreligious. The Sufis seem to "get it" more than your run of the mill Christian, whatever that means. The people who seem to really get something from religion have an ecstatic experience. They don't need rational demonstration, and those that contemplate divinity might even say that God is just an unknowable idea that we toss out there as a stand-in for actual divinity (mystery). Joseph Campbell would certainly have us think so.

In other words, Sufis (or etc) have a direct experience of ecstasy that requires no logical rationale. But the underlying postulate falls outside the scope of scientific inquiry. The only reason why this question is of any importance is because beliefs can be organizing principles, in regard to how we mentally construct and then experience the world around us. Our orientation toward existence changes based on our understanding of it, though it's not actually our orientation towards physics that seems important. (In terms of seeing how a Voudon or Sufi lives as opposed to an Athiest).

Though the beliefs of religion may appear man-made (certainly Ludwig Feuerbach made a solid claim to that effect in the *Essence of Christianity*, and it is a central theme in Nietzsche's discussion of religion), Science too is man-made, though when it comes to the mechanics of the natural world, it is very effective at getting us out of the picture–at least to an extent. Let's not forget the number of scientists that were theists of one sort or another. The scientific mind isn't incapable of religious experience.

The unknowable, some of the central questions of existence, are not answerable through science. To do so is to put absolute faith in logic, and in the conclusions we have drawn from it today rather than tomorrow, which is something the failure of the Enlightenment project should have put to rest.

Science is an iterative method which functions best in the absence of belief, though it's arguable Scientists develop their own forms of religious fervor. Religion is a means by which individual is linked to society to divinity. One is an instrument of empirical discovery and verification, the other, a social institution or personal relationship between an individual and their own understanding of the divine.

> *Just through looking at the etymology of the word, we can see this. "Religion" comes from the Latin religiō, religiōn-, perhaps from religāre, "to tie fast." Note that the meaning of this word is fundamentally the same as the meaning of the Sanskrit word Yoga, literally "union, yoking," or "to join." In both cases it is an attempt at joining the reference, which the religion refers to but cannot in itself embody, the social body, and the individual. This "joining" may also apply to the social body of the religion, though it is usually through the imposition of social dynamics that the religion polarizes into its opposite, and atrocities (holy wars as with the Crusades, bloody in-fighting over interpretation as with the Protestants, inquisitions, etc.), occur.* **The Immanence of Myth.**

Even a belief in God seems secondary (especially in many Eastern systems) in comparison to that psychological or social function. Literal belief in God also isn't prerequisite for religious experience to arise. This is something really worth considering.

Personally, I'm more interested in how belief effects behavior and experience than in whether or not that belief is real. (It can be dangerous, however, if we believe that things that aren't real are, or vice versa.) I suppose this is an anthropological perspective. I am essentially an agnostic on this matter, because that's what absolute honesty demands. What bothers me is the arrogance that says that someone else's experience is wrong, yours is right, and furthermore, those people are clearly idiots because they don't see x, y, and z, when z is by definition unknowable. That problem exists for many theists and atheists alike. The bravest thing can be to admit what surpasses the capacities of universal reason and experience.

Unfortunately, it's improbable if not impossible that a discussion like this can possibly sway anyone who has already made up their minds about these matters. Atheists and theists are alike in their certainty, unable to consider anything that doesn't directly follow from the presupposed postulates of their belief. On this issue, it is probably best to remain silent.

Debunking the New World Order Mythology

Rusty Shackleford

"When you define the power elite as somebody else, I regard that as a loser's script. I define the power elite as myself and my friends." **Robert Anton Wilson**

Lately, the hive mind has been crackling with transmissions via blogs and social networking regarding fascism and corporate police states, abuses of power, and notions, some of which are realistic and some of which clearly aren't, as to who is *responsible.*

Listen: What I am about to tell you may sting, but there is no "New World Order," other than you. You, yourself. You are the New World Order, you are the conspiracy, for better or for worse.

Allow me to explain.

According to New Age myth, the Hopi Indians predicted that there would be a fifth age. This new age they termed the age of "spirit" or of "ether." According to their timeline, and also the timeline of the Mayans, December 21, 2012 is roughly the spot in which the current age we are inhabiting transitions into something radically different. Or so we are told.

The Hindu people termed the age in which we currently live to be the Kali Yuga. Traditionally, this is viewed by many people to be negative but in the grand scheme of things it is a stepping stone or transitional period to a new age. The Kali Yuga itself refers to a period in which humanity is preoccupied with greed, spiritual ignorance, superstition, bigotry and emotional poverty. Conquering seems to be the overall goal, and multiplying and replicating without any real motive other than to grow and to consume (much like a cancer) seems to be the overriding value of human conduct.

Enter 2012. Many are already aware of the Mayan prophecies concerning a new era, but some may be unaware of the possible correlation between this and what the Vedic scriptures considered to be the dawn of a new "Golden Age" for humanity. This new age was predicted to be the end of the Kali Yuga or the age of iron and the beginning of the new Golden Dawn of enlightenment for humanity.

Alternately, we see the Hopi Indians predicting much of the same, although there is an admonition and a warning: We collectively as a species can choose to make this "new age" one of enlightenment, one of freedom and beauty, or we can choose to further descend into bickering, extremely polarized left or right wing political ideology, petty in-fighting and bigotry (religious or otherwise.)

I want to pose a series of questions to the more radical extremists of the so-called "NWO Conspiracy Theory" camp. Firstly, have you listened to someone like Alex Jones speak at length? Does this man not appear to you to be a stark raving mad paranoid lunatic? This is not an *ad hominem* attack, listen to him speak (or rather, scream unintelligibly and menace people with boogiemen to boost his ratings and keep them feeling powerless and fearful.) THE EMPEROR WEARS NO CLOTHES.

Secondly, do you really believe with the level of incompetency which the Western world, and the world at large, seems to be governed, that there is some grand conspiracy at work? Wouldn't it be more simple to assume that the basic conspiracy at work here is human greed, stupidity and tyranny? Does this have to take the form of flying saucers from planet X or shape-shifting reptilians?

Perhaps it is in the vested interest of those who would control your behavior to think that you are in fact powerless and that you have no say, and that they are really shape-shifting Annunaki reptilian gods from the planet Nibiru... (Who knows, maybe they really are. Francis Crick, the acid head who won the Nobel Prize for discovering the double helix DNA coil, was himself obsessed with the notion that human beings were genetically modified via. Extraterrestrial intervention.)

Nevertheless, here is something that has rarely steered me wrong throughout my life, and I hope that it will help you: Occam's razor, better known as the law of parsimony. If common sense dictates that the people who seem to be in charge are just fuckups, perpetually clumsy and overprivileged children playing at cowboys and Indians, the chances are they are just that. Let's not make something out of nothing. The simplest of explanations is usually the best. Again, THE EMPEROR WEARS NO CLOTHES.

As I have hinted at before, I am in fact a "member" of a "spiritual organization," of sorts. Just exactly which is not important. What I will tell you is this: I have sworn to myself to make it my work to fight for human liberty and freedom, and am vehemently opposed to the forces of superstition and tyranny. I am not rich (I am presently below the poverty line), nor am I a member of the Council on Foreign Relations. I have not nor do I ever intend on attending the "Cremation of Dull Care" ceremonies of the Bohemian Grove Club, which have enlisted bands such as The Grateful Dead to perform for them.

The Bohemian Grove Club, incidentally, seems to be really little more than a game of grabass for rich white men that is itself reminiscent of Burning Man, only a little less corporate and minus the hot hippie chicks. They even set a giant statue on fire. Total sausage fest. (Hey, Rich Queer Politicians & Bankers have to get their kicks too, you know? Maybe "we" are not so different, after all.)

And herein lies the crux of the matter: Ignorance and the veil of Maya or illusion tells us that we are separate.

"He has more money than me. I don't trust him."

"He is a Mason, we all know they are the evil conspirators that control the banks."

"She looks different. I don't like the way she wears her makeup or her hair colored like that."

"He is a Christian, I am a Muslim."

"He is a Catholic, and I am a protestant. His Christ is not the same as MINE."

"I don't like cops."

Symbols divide us, too. How many times have you heard people say these things to justify not taking the time to get to know someone for who they really are without resorting to stereotypes and shifting the blame onto them for all of the world's ills? This is known as the "parental conspiracy." All of the world's problems as you perceive them could not *possibly* begin and end with you yourself. So you have to find other people, the CFR, the Masons, the Jesuits, the Jews, the Bankers, the Illuminati, Mom, Dad, the mayor, the Goddamned Gnomes of Zurich on which to blame your problems.

This is not to say that there aren't legitimate conspiracies, and that there are not those who hold positions of physical or temporal power abusing this power and exploiting other human beings. There most certainly are, and will continue to be. We should do our best as citizens and human beings to hold these persons accountable and to keep them from taking advantage of us as much as possible. That does not mean there is a grand conspiracy at work. Can you imagine a group of selfish, childish, ignorant and greedy human beings agreeing to cooperate on much of anything for more than a few years at a time, let alone hundreds of years? This seems to me to be damned near impossible.

Think about it.

Don't bitch about the media. Become the media. Be who you are, uncompromisingly so and don't worry about the consequences. Do this and you will receive much less resistance than otherwise, and in fact you may begin to find that people respect you more. If they do not respect you, they will hate you, or perhaps better yet fear you... In which case, you are still influencing them more than if you just kept your mouth shut and kept your real thoughts to yourself. Try an experiment: See if you can go a whole day being as uncompromisingly honest as you can. See and take note of how uncomfortable it makes the people around you, who more often than not are not used to human beings acting with integrity and being forthcoming in social settings. Better yet, try this social experiment: See if you can go a whole day without trying to make the people around you comfortable. You may be amazed at how difficult this can be!

Bottom line: We *are* the changes occurring within both the macro and micro scales of human development and evolution. Before we point the finger again, we should learn that our best chance of survival as individuals and as a species will be to consciously seek more light and to learn to roll with these changes as opposed to fighting them. This does not mean let people walk all over you and don't hold those who abuse their political or financial power accountable. This means, put down the hash pipe for a minute and go do something that will change the world. Agonizing over whether or not the Bavarian Illuminati rule the world along with the CFR, the Trilateral Commission, the Free Masons, the Bilderbirgers, the Jews, the Swiss Bankers, the Knights of Malta, the Gnomes of Zurich, the Knights Templar and any other convenient scapegoat you can find will not set you free.

We are the New World Order. We are these changes. We can choose to make the new age an age of beauty and enlightenment and a spiritual utopia, or we can choose to remain in darkness. And it is a choice that you yourself have the power to make. Do not let anyone convince you otherwise.

Rusty Shackelford is a tragic wreck of a human being. But in his slow motion self-immolation, he has helped many young adults attain enlightenment.

Into The Hyper-Real I

Census Sweep

Cat Vincent

It's always an odd sensation to discover that a field of interest you've passionate about but know is considered fringe at best has been under the scrutiny of academia for some time.

I first learned about the work of Australian sociologist Dr. Adam Possamai from the excellent Theofantastique blog which covers the intersection of religion and cinema. Drawing on the work of Baudrillard, Possamai coined the term "hyper-real religion" to describe the post-modern, syncretic belief systems that have arisen from pop culture. One major example he mentions is Jediism.

I've always been drawn to the way people can gain spiritual and mystical perspectives from avowedly fictional works. Some of my most intense moments of gnosis have sprung from certain movies and TV shows. So, I've no problem at all with this. Others, it is clear, do.

Though plenty of people have been feeling a spiritual connection with Star Wars since 1977, the framing of this into an actual denomination didn't really come up until the UK census of 2001, where a grass-roots campaign managed to get 390,000 participants to put Jedi as their religion. (This was the first UK census to ask the religion question– it had tick-boxes for the major Judaeo-Christian flavours, Hinduism, "None" and a fill-in box for "Other.") These figures put Jediism into the position of 4th most prevalent faith in the UK, above Judaism, Sikhism and Buddhism, and way above Paganism.

Of course, many if not most of these entries were frankly taking the piss– and the authorities responded, by putting specific codicils into religious protection legislation exempting Jediism (along with two another sci-fi faiths, Scientology and Satanism) from discrimination protection in law. Nonetheless...

As I've noted elsewhere, the Jedi have made some inroads towards official recognition– as in the case of a Jedi who went into a Job Centre, was asked to lower his hood, refused on religious grounds– and was forced to leave, only to complain and be issued a formal apology for insulting his faith. This happened at the same time as a Christian nurse losing her discrimination law suit when she was disciplined for refusing to stow her crucifix when on duty.

(And don't even get me started on how keeping your hood raised as a Jedi isn't even canon...)

It's census time again here in Blighty. The Jedi are again pushing for inclusion. And there's a strong push against them, from *atheists*.

Noted geek pundit Cory Doctorow jokingly tweeted his family might put Jedi on the 2011 census form religion option– he was instantly barraged by aggrieved atheists from the already-extant You Are Not A Jedi campaign, leading to a placating post on BoingBoing– a site which gets more than a few hits.

What interests me about all this– and has been the subject of Possamai's scholarly-yet-sympathetic gaze– is the question of *what defines a religion that must be taken seriously*?

Is it longevity? If so, then most American evangelical faiths are less than a century old, as are neo-paganism, Baha'i and of course Scientology.

Is it numbers? "Judge me by my size, do you?"

Is it how many of your avowed believers are sincere in their belief? It's a criticism getting specifically aimed at Jediism, as noted above– but an awful lot of folk just say they're Christian or whatever out of habit or societal pressure. How does one measure religious sincerity, exactly?

Is it the historical evidence of their roots? That would rule out pretty much all Bible-based beliefs, unless you're a xtian-biased archaeologist.

Is it power and influence? Scientology has forced a position in the US of considerable prestige, but it's nowhere near as 'respected' elsewhere.

And, most relevantly here– **is it knowing the source material is unquestionably, undeniably fictional?**

An atheist would make a very sincere case that all religions are based on fiction. Most observers outside of a faith would note that, however "real" its roots, all belief systems pick up a bit of fictionalising– mythologising, in the narrow sense– along the way.

So the question is: *who decides*?

Belief is as personal a thing as there is. And in many, it varies– shifting from knee-jerk to utter belief to doubt. In some, it's based on a personal mythology taken from life experience and ideas taken from every source, even fiction– the often-maligned "pick and mix" syncreticism. Why exactly do people who claim their faith is unwavering, unquestioned and ineffably (in their minds) *true* get privileged above those whose faith is fluid, Mercurial? Is it really just because it's easier to put on a form?

I'm putting Taoist on my census form. It's pretty close, and allows the possibility that what I believe is only a symbol of the numinous– in short, it leaves room for flexibility, without actually lying.

But what about the sincere Jedi– or Na'Vi or Discordian (if there can be such a thing)? Does a religion having an origin in taking the piss out of another religion, or the religious impulse itself, exempt it from being taken seriously? Though the Church of the Flying Spaghetti Monster started as a reductio-ab-absurdam of xtian evolutionary theory, it's occupying enough mindspace that some, I am sure, are quite sincere when they call for the blessing of His Noodly Appendage.

The Church of All Worlds, derived from Heinlein's *Stranger in a Strange Land*, has been a feature in SF fandom since the 60s and I've been in situations where sharing water became an unquestionably sincere mystical act.

I don't have all the answers– hell, I've barely started to form the right questions. Adam Possamai's work asks a lot of interesting ones that I'd not considered, and I'll talk about some of those here later. Next, I'll be looking at how the hyper-real faiths can be seen as *product*, as an offshoot of late-capitalism– and whether or not this makes them (and possibly all modern beliefs) cargo cults.

POSTSCRIPT:

The British Humanist Association has tried, unsuccessfully, to have posters about their position re: the census appear at British railway stations. In a piece on the subject at christian.org.uk, the following appeared:

The forthcoming census and the BHA's campaign were featured on Radio 4's Sunday programme this week.

Speaking on the programme, BHA chief executive Andrew Copson said the religion question in the census was "aberrantly imprecise" and "wantonly inaccurate."

He said the results of the census would lead government, both nationally and locally, to make "wrong assumptions" based on "erroneous data" when allocating resources and developing policies.

But a Church of England spokesperson disagreed with his criticism.

Revd Linda Barley, Head of the Church of England's Research and Statistics Department, said of the religion question: "It's not about belonging, it's not about believing, it's not about practice, or any of those things, it's about just whether people feel they align themselves with different religious persuasions."

She went on to say that the kind of more detailed information Andrew Copson was looking for would come from surveys like the British Social Attitudes Survey "to find out what it means on the ground."

And her comments were backed by Peter Benton, Deputy Director of the 2011 Census.

"There are different concepts that you can measure in relation to religion", he said, including religious practice, belief and affiliation.

"And when we've talked to the people that use the census data", he added, "the one that matters most to them is religious affiliation".

He concluded: "we could have chosen to measure some of the narrower aspects but it was a deliberate decision not to."

If the definition of someone claiming a faith-identity comes down to "whether or not people feel they align themselves with different religious persuasions", then how does any belief, fiction-based or not, fail to qualify?

Cat Vincent used to fight bad weird shit professionally as a paranormal security consultant and director of Athanor Consulting. He retired from field work in January 2009ce, but continues writing and blogging about mysticism, the occult and edge philosophies.

Into The Hyper-real II

Cargo Cult

Cat Vincent

One of the key perspectives in the work of Adam Possamai in regard to the 'hyper-real' postmodern pop-culture belief systems comes from his background as a sociologist. As a result of this, he frames a lot of his analysis of the phenomenon as manifestations of late-capitalism. Put simply, he sees them on one level as *product*.

He's got a point. Pop culture, by definition, is something we can buy. (Or steal, or bootleg... but I'll get to that later.) It's a manifestation of mass production and dissemination. It's worship of things you can buy in a shop. Production line totems.

In other words, like a cargo cult.

In the South Seas there is a cargo cult of people. During the war they saw airplanes land with lots of good materials, and they want the same thing to happen now. So they've arranged to imitate things like runways, to put fires along the sides of the runways, to make a wooden hut for a man to sit in, with two wooden pieces on his head like headphones and bars of bamboo sticking out like antennas– he's the controller– and they wait for the airplanes to land. They're doing everything right. The form is perfect. It looks exactly the way it looked before. But it doesn't work. No airplanes land. So I call these things cargo cult science, because they follow all the apparent precepts and forms of scientific investigation, but they're missing something essential, because the planes don't land. **Richard Feynman.**

The last remaining cargo cult, the worship of a semi-mythical (possibly black US Army soldier) John Frum is on the South Sea island of Tanna. It's well worth reading Mike Jay's 2002 piece on the history and current state of the Vanatu who worship Frum. Jay finds the history of Frum-worship rife with meaning and symbolism for our times.

Frum is a mercurial figure– a Jesus/Moses/Spartacus figure, who has inspired automatically-received songs in languages the Vanatu do not speak. One of my favourite stories of the Frum-inspired rebellion against colonial rule, told by Jay, goes:

...by 1941 there was no doubt that something was going on. A "prophet" named Manehevi from Sulphur Bay had been arrested and tied to a tree for a day by the colonial administration, pour encourager les autres, but John Frum continued to appear. Subsequent witnesses had been deported and imprisoned. Then, big news: a huge detachment of American troops had arrived on the neighbouring island of Santo. Not only had these Americans brought unheard-of amounts of cargo– arms, tanks, boats, food, medicine - but a considerable number of them were black. The centuries of unbroken symmetry between foreigners (white, rich) and locals (black, poor) had been broken, and the black GIs were variously interpreted as descendants of the islanders who'd been kidnapped by plantation owners in the past, or as John Frum's own detachment of the US army. Messianic fervour gripped Sulphur Bay, and one Sunday morning the new movement came out into the open with a baffling act of civil disobedience which sent shock-waves through the white community. The compulsory attendance at the Presbyterian church was universally ignored; instead, a group of locals walked solemnly into the white-owned trading post and carefully removed every price label from the stock.

That last touch, the peaceful occupation of a symbol of the privileged of capitalism struck me as awfully similar to the approach taken by the UK Uncut affinity group, who protested the draconian public service cuts in Britain by a peaceful sit-in at one of London's poshest shops, Fortnum and Mason.

All 150-odd non-violent activists caused no more damage than knocking over a chocolate Easter bunny (symbolic sacrifice?) and were tricked out of the building by police– told they were being moved for their protection, then nicked as soon as they were out.

A couple of days after that action, I first read the Mike Jay piece, and today I read this: Islands at the Speed of Light, at BLDGBLOG:

A recent paper published in the Physical Review *has some astonishing suggestions for the geographic future of financial markets. Its authors, Alexander Wissner-Grossl and Cameron Freer, discuss the spatial implications of speed-of-light trading. Trades now occur so rapidly, they explain, and in such fantastic quantity, that the speed of light itself presents limits to the efficiency of global computerized trading networks.*

These limits are described as "light propagation delays."

It is thus in traders' direct financial interest, they suggest, to install themselves at specific points on the earth's surface– a kind of light-speed financial acupuncture– in order to take advantage both of the planet's geometry and of the networks along which trades are ordered and filled. They conclude that "the construction of relativistic statistical arbitrage trading nodes across the Earth's surface" is thus economically justified, if not required.

Amazingly, though, their analysis suggests that many of these financially strategic points are actually out in the middle of nowhere: hundreds of miles offshore in the Indian Ocean, for instance, on the shores of Antarctica, and scattered throughout the South Pacific– though, of course, most of Europe, Japan, and the U.S. Bos-Wash corridor also make the cut.

These nodes exist in what the authors refer to as "the past light cones" of distant trading centers– thus the paper's multiple references to relativity. Astonishingly, this thus seems to elide financial trading networks with the laws of physics, implying the eventual emergence of what we might call quantum financial products. Quantum derivatives! (This also seems to push us ever closer to the artificially intelligent financial instruments described in Charles Stross's novel *Accelerando*).

It's financial science fiction: when the dollar value of a given product depends on its position in a planet's light-cone.

Wouldn't it be interesting if one of those financial Feng-shui nodes just happened to be on or near Tanna? If the actual control of the world's cargo were to flow through Frum's land? There's also the distinct possibility of quasi-national libertarian states, like the late lamented Sealand, could pop up too.

John Frum versus John Galt?

The control, both financially and possibly magically, of the products of late capitalism, caught in our local light cone, distributed at lightspeed. The swiftest of the messengers of the gods of cargo.

One of these products of late capitalism, a comic book produced by the Time-Warner/DC empire (specifically Neil Gaiman's *Sandman*), once suggested that *all* human religions are cargo cults. It's a throwaway idea, what Gaiman himself called a "notion" rather than a fully-fledged idea. But it's one that stuck with me, because the language of commerce and trade has infiltrated everything. We talk metaphorically of the cost of our actions, the price we have to pay, the deals we must strike. The death toll of a military action, in British military slang, is called the Butcher's Bill. And England, let us not forget, was described by Napoleon as a nation of shopkeepers. And if England are shopkeepers, what then are Americans?

One of the biggest ever US pop-culture influences world-wide is undoubtedly Star Trek. And it's really interesting to me that the show makes a point of saying that a precondition of their relatively utopian and egalitarian society is that "we outgrew the need for money"... without actually telling us how they did so. Further, when Star Trek's later iterations appeared, this was underlined further by the appearance of a culture which far more closely resembles the character of modern capitalist society than the enlightened Federation... the Ferengi. (It's notable and ironic that the name Ferengi derives from the Arabic/Persian word for foreigner...)

Possamai, I must note, is scrupulously fair about the way capitalism influences faith. He notes how there's an opposite reaction to the hyper-real religions– a kind of hypo-real fundamentalist pushback, limiting the faithful's access to a 'free market' of ideas, offering narrow but plentiful products of their own. It's perfectly possible for a child to be, for example, raised, educated and employed entirely within a climate of Xtian Dominionism– they have their own books, toys, TV shows, internet realms, pop music, comics– all the things the hyper-real draws on, but neutered, made acceptable within their paradigm. And it's almost too obvious to note how their megachurches increasingly resemble corporations, their temples more and more like malls.

And the Chaotes, the Newagers of every stripe, the Na'Vi and the Jedi and the FSMites... all work their ways, buy the albums and books and DVDs and action figures and How To Speak Klingon CDs, many of them deeply suspicious of just how that cargo ends up in their hands. As suspicious as the Vanatu, with no John Frum to lead them.

So, knowing all this: how's a denizen of the Capitalist, English-speaking West to react? How do we find our spiritual, mythic and magical place within these mass-produced possibilities?

I'll take a look at that next time.

Into The Hyper-real III

Modern Soul

Cat Vincent

Gypsies, tramps and thieves,

You hear it from the people of the town, they call us

Gypsies, tramps and thieves…

But every night, the men would come around,

And lay their money down.

Sonny and Cher.

The question I left with last time was;

If, as the work of Adam Possamai suggests, modern culture (and pop-culture especially) is essentially a product of the machinations of late-capitalism, is just *product*, merely *cargo*, then what can we, supposedly nothing more than mere consumers, do to find a relevant personal spirituality?

The answer to that lays somewhere in the nature of power, ownership and control.

It's clear that the modern industrial West is a place where the definition of ownership and property is getting… blurry. Corporations benefit on the one hand from immense political influence which they use to redefine the concept of property– swapping actual ownership of sold goods to a model where the consumer merely rents them from 'the cloud', to suing anyone who infringes 'their' copyright while plundering other cultures and counter-cultures for their next Big Idea– and, on the other, from the trillions given to them to bail out economies fractured by the biggest Ponzi scheme in human history…

From which they also profited to the sum of trillions of dollars. Numbers and power like that have a crushing weight to them, a force of gravity like supermassive black holes in culture.

So perhaps the best way to deal with them is to turn that gravity against them, to slingshot past their aims and, gaining speed from their mass, plunge ever deeper into imaginal space.

And, as we pass, steal anything that isn't nailed down.

A key concept here is the Situationist term *Détournement* and the parallel idea of *Bricolage*– the taking of the products of capitalism and inverting them, remaking them to serve people rather than be cargo-trinkets to be worshiped and sought.

Think: remix culture, sampling, cut-ups, mash-ups. Sharing, rather than unequal 'free' market trading. Pirate Bay. Fan-fic and Adbusters. Open-source Makers rather than trademark-and-copyrighted sellers. Stealing back from the thieves.

The Street finding it's own use for things.

It's not like there's a lack of examples of popular ground-level belief systems appropriating the symbols and tools of the mainstream for their own purposes– from the John Frum devotees I mentioned last time, to Voudon altars covered with cigars, cheap bottles of rum and shop-bought Virgin Mary devotional candles. So many stories, so many tools, *why not* just pick them up, wield them– and most importantly, see what they can do when you *ignore the warranty,* use them outside of the realm of the manufacturer's warning?

Ever wondered why Hermes was the god of both magicians and thieves? Why *crafty* has nuances of meaning that imply both skill and cunning? Why bricolage derives from the French word for a tinker? *It's a hint.*

The biggest confidence trick of our times is that we are nothing but powerless, passive consumers. That this is not only how things should be, but that it's good for us. But we can and should be more– active, smart, crafty tool-users. Tinkers, and tinkerers. The master's tools bloody well *can* be used to dismantle (or rebuild) the master's house– that's what tools are *for.* Turn the con back on the grifters. Provide leverage.

Possamai calls this kind of attitude towards the old myths and models 'Presentist Perrenism'– which, "even though it borrows eclectically from earlier esotericism, is to be understood as an expression, in the field of spirituality, of emergent post-industrial or post-modern culture."

The side-effect of all that individualism that has been pushed as a way to make us buy newer and shinier things as a 'lifestyle choice' has had the unintended consequence of letting 'consumers' actually make those same individual choices *about their own natures*– and use the tools and themes and memes that array around them as the means to develop and construct their own path, their own mythos. The refusal to accept that anyone has the right to define our personal mythology but *ourselves* is an increasingly radical act, especially in the face of violently competing resurgent great narratives, dualistic us-and-them battles. There is far more to be had at the margins, the bordertowns; the messy and vibrant meniscus between buyer and seller, adherent and heretic, the economists and the economised.

All the fun stuff happens at the edges: where the carnival shows and travelling clans, the car-boot sales and swap-mets, set up. Beyond the Pale. Beyond the consensus definition of the Real... out in the Hyperreal. Where the mages, fanboys and roleplayers, the short-con men and the jugglers, the makers and the hackers and the rest of the Tribe of the Strange live, where it's not quite safe and certainly not at all respectable or ordered or polite– and especially not Business As Usual. Where myth lives again.

I hope to see you there.

Amondawa

Timeless and Without Rapture

David Metcalfe

A recent article on the BBC News website details the investigation of an Amazonian tribe called the Amondawa who don't make any linguistic distinctions between time and space. Lacking temporal concepts applied to space, as the article points out, makes statements like "study through the night" linguistically impossible. This is in some ways an expression of the awareness engendered by taboo as discussed in a previous essay on Modern Mythology, Where Nature Lies Naked Awaiting the Hunt. Writing on the day of Harold Camping's predictions of immanent Rapture the power of language to control the cultural narrative is rarely so pointed.

For the Amondawa the concept of a Rapture would be impossible to express. There can be no rectification of time and space, spirit and matter, eternity and finitude, when the two are not separated in the first place.

As Chris Sinha, a professor of psychology of language at the University of Portsmouth, describes in the article, "What we don't find is a notion of time as being independent of the events which are occurring; they don't have a notion of time which is something the events occur in." A simple linguistic lack completely reconfigures the possibilities of the cultural narrative. Lacking a word for time, the Amondawa cannot anticipate an End of Time, and by not relating temporal and spacial concepts through a division they cannot have an End of Days.

The Rapture as understood by Camping is based on Dispensational Premillenialism, the awkward child of 19th century rationalism uneasily married to Judeo-Christian visionary texts. It is a mytho-mathematical theory based on a literal and temporal understanding of the Judeo-Christian tradition. For the most part this is all much more useful as fuel for infographic abandon than deep theological engagement.

Here the return of the Messiah is seen in multiple stages in which believers physically enter Eternity prior to the culmination of the End of Time. Time and Eternity continue to coexist in the interim between the two events which are both assumed to be at a certain distance in the future from the present time. The crux of the entire program is firmly rooted in materialism, from the means of the ascension of the chosen to the heaven into which they ascend.

With the current reaction against Intelligent Design, Creationism and other heterodox materialist theories loosely based on Christianity, concepts such as the Rapture seem a bit absurd to many people. Unfortunately the same relationship between time and space that allows for 19th century Rationalism to transmute Judeo-Christian visionary texts into pulp fiction tropes also protect ideas like Progress, Evolution, space exploration and utopian theories such as the Singularity and New Age narratives.

Western civilization is fueled by the longing for some transcendent moment that will heal our compounding ills. Hidden beneath nearly every layer of culture are concepts just as shaky as Camping's ideas of the Second Coming. The sense of timelessness that the Amondawa have due to the structure of their language has been the bane of Western expansion for centuries.

When there is no sense of time, no possibility for a culmination of time, there is no impetuous for consumption. As Kali teaches so perfectly, Time and Death are intimately acquainted, and Death in its many guises is the most potent tool any advertiser, activist, marketer, propagandist, leader or judiciary can wield. When the devotee finds Kali, Time and Death cease to exist as opposition becomes union.

Without Death there is no end to pleasure, thus no excess or need to over indulge. Without excess there is no lack, therefore there can be no debt, and no one in debt to another. Take away the word Time and you unseat the entire program of Western civilization.

Both Capitalism and Marxism have their secular Raptures, the faithful taken up into the Utopian ideal of wealth in perpetuum mobile or equilateral distribution. In either case stasis, and thus Timelessness, are achieved. The Amondawa have no Adam Smith, no Karl Marx.

The Amondawa also escape the binding power of the progressive myths that Smith and Marx created to sustain continued development of Western civilization. Without that ever elusive end-point, there is no reason to keep going forward.

We continue to be fascinated by Camping's Rapture, 2012, Atlantis, utopia and so many other narratives because the Amondawa exist. We need a Time killer, a culmination, a story that explains how we return to *forgetfulness of Time*. In all of our movement, however, there is always the sneaking suspicion that we may in fact be standing still. What the Amondawa teach us is that it's much easier than all that. There's no need for complex metaphysical acrobatics, it's as simple as forgetting a word. Isn't it?

The Snare of Distance

and the Sunglasses of the Seer

Brian George

And, spread across solemn distances, your smile entered my heart. **Rilke**

I recently posted an essay on Reality Sandwich called "The Vanguard of a Perpetual Revolution." In the forum for this essay, Okantomi wrote, "I often feel like I can see what is happening in the world, as well as what is just about to happen, and what will almost certainly happen later on, and it's like no one else sees what I am seeing. It's eerie, shocking, and finally depressing."

People do have visions of the future, both individually and collectively. Hollywood blockbusters, for example– *Star Wars, Terminator, Blade Runner, Total Recall, Lord of the Rings, Avatar*– strike me as one of the most potent forms of contemporary myth-making, in which the ancient world resurfaces as a technological dream on the horizon. Seized from afar, as by the magnetism of an almost nonexistent teacher, we are pulled by a current all too eager to instruct us. An unresolved agenda speaks to us from the screen. The screen also acts like an iron curtain, through which the bodies of the living may not pass. Or, in a different mode, people give form to the future through their fears, by all of those things that we know but go out of our way not to think about: that reserves of oil will almost certainly run out in our lifetimes, that the US doesn't manufacture much of anything anymore, and that there is very little locally grown food– not enough to sustain a major city in the case of a real emergency.

There are many things that it seems better not to know.

The future is one of the better places in which to store such unasked for knowledge.

The problem is, of course, to separate and categorize these alternate versions of the future– in simplistic terms, to discriminate between the more false than true and the more true than false.

Sadly, there are laws that prevent our switching out of power save, in order to reactivate the full scope of our senses. The art of remote viewing is no longer taught in schools. Bilocation is now seen as unscientific. From their underground bases– speeding all ways at once, like boomerangs, and with superhuman stealth– bad UFOs play games with the horizon.

Fear and hope pump out a kind of metaphysical fog, crackling with static, which makes every level of the process difficult, and tests our ability to read what is beyond our imagination.

Through the years, and especially in the early 1990s, I have frequently found myself projected into the future– both in terms of specific images and through wider visionary overviews. References to the destruction of the World Trade Towers popped up five or six times in poems from 1992. "A monster stalked his head through the air vents of the World Trade Towers." The World Trade Towers for a fourth time fall; their shadows stand." There were other lines from this period that possibly pointed to the Gulf oil disaster: "The sea has met its death by accident." And to Fukushima: "You have thrown a wave at the reactors of the Nephillim."

There were dozens of references in my books "To Akasha/ Parts 1 and 2" to the idea of a 1-mile wave or a mile-high wave. "To Akasha/ Part 1" was structured around this image, and it was a phrase that I never expected to hear in the news. But, during the Gulf oil crisis, reporters began to speak about what would happen if the vast lakes of methane under the Gulf were to explode. Once consequence of this would be a mile-high wave that would wash over two thirds of North America.

As Okantomi suggests, prophecy may have less to do with the prediction of the future than with the ability to see clearly into the present– to boldly recognize patterns that are just beginning to be formed or to probe into patterns that have long been in existence, but which, for whatever reason, have not yet become visible. For the most part, this involves a set of classical virtues rather than a bag of supernatural powers. Among the most important of these virtues are: the ability to step back, the subtlety to be more empathic even as your detachment grows, a capacity, while still in love with life, to be dead, and a willingness to stand on your own as you free yourself from the force-fields of the common wisdom. Even good habits must be probed and then, finally, dismantled. All crutches must be thrown away, as you free yourself from the advice of experts, from the emotions roused by the desire to see your side win and the other side destroyed, and from the hypnotic fixations generated by the media.

Conversely, you must have the courage to accept that you do not, in fact, create your own reality. For the "You" is inextricably bound to the experience of the "We." The "Body Politic" is an actual body– however much we might choose to view it as a metaphor. You are one of 6 ½ 7 billion being swept along through the veins of a metastasizing empire, whose reach is inter-dimensional in its scope, but whose key principle, at the moment, is nowhere to be found. Its search engines troll for evidence that it has not ceased to exist– as there, just up ahead, the ghosts of super-beings beckon from the fallout.

If we are a storehouse for the "seeds of every form and the sprouts of every sort of life," as Pico della Mirandola argued, and if the One that we are does not depend upon the image that we project, holographically, and towards some particular end, who knows but that we might not scare ourselves? "The New Man is living amongst us now! He is here!" said Hitler, "Isn't that enough for you? I will tell you a secret. I have seen the New Man. He is intrepid and cruel. Even I was afraid of him." Once, we were not so easily impressed. We had not yet volunteered to be eaten by the gods– they to whom we had given birth.

Much stupider than they think, Earth's top one percent are adept at playing games. Let us posit: That they rule by reactivating some Antediluvian trauma, the fear of which has been bred into our bones, the records about which have been hidden in the coils of junk DNA, which they, and they alone, have somehow learned to read. Such feats of micromanagement! All data is then made to correspond. "As you are figuring out the world," they say, "we will have manufactured a new one, and then another one after that!" This does not mean that they are actually in charge. Like us, they are subject to whatever spells they cast, and, as the apparatus of the Great Year turns, they are swept along with the other 99 percent. No part can ever be taken from the whole, nor does the One increase when added to itself. We move as One– unconsciously, and pushed forward from behind.

As we free ourselves from the common wisdom, paranoia may be the most immediate of temptations. All conspiracy theories may be true, or none of them, or a fact from this one and an archetype from that one, but in the end such labyrinthine explorations may not lead to greater freedom. The trap is this: That we are always the good guys, and someone else is always to blame for every evil in the world.

Appearances to the contrary, it is possible that the things that matter most are actually very simple. As citizens of the greater city of the cosmos, who have now been grounded, it is our job to remove the layers of obfuscation that cut each person from the core of his/her power, so that each may again serve as a kind of movable Omphalos. Gently but persistently, we must bring our attention back to what I will call the Boy Scout (or Girl Scout) virtues. Among these are: love of acting well for its own sake, honesty, courage, compassion, a willingness to work hard, stick-to-it-iveness, curiosity, a sense of proportion, a sense of justice, generosity, a willingness to meet each person on his or her own terms, a balance of self-assertion and humility, self-awareness, a willingness to take responsibility for one's actions, a willingness to admit that one is wrong, and what Hemingway called "a built-in bullshit detector."

We must be good little boys and girls– or else! But no: Instead these virtues will provide a launch pad from which memory may move freely in and out, pulling relics from behind the order of projection. As Lincoln said in his 1862 "Annual Message to Congress," "We must dis-enthrall ourselves." These virtues will allow us to stay grounded as we venture to reconstruct the non-dual architecture of the city, which exists in no one place. For observe, my wide-eyed shipmates, there is no such thing as Time, and the lightning bolt that directs us falls crazily where it will. The emptiness that is space shows no sign of disturbance. We cannot leave, for we never did exist, and in flashes, it now seems that the whole world is transparent– as are others, world after world.

Once, the Kundalini hid its teachings inside forms– as a test of whose skill in camouflage they served, and from whose potency they had been created. We must later on determine how to free them. We must harmonize the scalar energy that spills from the HARP technology of the Everyday Object.

Having once been set in motion, the Kundalini stirs up and expels a volcanic flux of images, as it burns through every obstacle in its path. It rips continents like sheets of paper. It dismantles the prosthetic bodies of the gods. It beams races from one side of the mirror to the other. It expunges every trace of the Antediluvian records, all arts and sciences, yet without even a small detail being lost. "But why is this necessary?" you might justifiably ask. It is possible that it does things just to show us that it can. Or, alternately, it is possible that our childhood is over, and that this circumstance presents us with a challenge: We must find a way to grow up. For there is no place that does not see you. Of limitation the master, perhaps this is the reason that you have allowed yourself to be blind.

At some point, cooling down, upon finding that there are no laws left to violate, the Kundalini may become much nicer than it was. Then as smoothly as a bell tone through the Zodiac, or as the arcing of a current through the ocean, it will move on to its predetermined end. Each atom will have 108 eyes.

We do not always have to be picked up and transported to view one dimension from the vantage point of another. A state of clarity will sometimes to the trick. Bypassing the need for hallucinatory display, we can glimpse just how the dimensions fit together, and why they interact as they do.

The world is almost infinitely complex, as is time, and human nature, but we should start by drawing a circle on the ground; we should place our feet at the center of a turning 10-dimensional torus, which can be statistically re-normalized as a circle no more than 10 feet wide– a circle that will be powered by our breath, and whose centripetal vortex will then gather up what it needs: Visions are allowed to visit, but fears and traumas and hatreds and projections will be required stand a few feet off. A standing wave will lead us to the center of the sun, inside of which are cities. Back home, in the center of the circle, we will find that our bio-energetic vehicles have been transformed into stones. At first worshiped by the masses, they will later come to be seen as normal parts of the environment. In passing, we will note that a day takes 24,000 years.

Hieroglyphs as well as geometric networks will spontaneously rearrange themselves. Thus "we will walk on the ruins of a vast sky," as Yves Bonnefoy said, and access, without moving, the databanks of space.

We must start from where we are, and trust in our own direct powers of perception. If we know– with close to 100 percent certainty– that there will be earthquakes in an earthquake zone, then we will know that this is not the ideal place to build a chain of nuclear power plants. We will laugh as we stare in wonderment at the expert who would disagree. If we know that all reserves of oil are to give out in our lifetimes, whereupon our way of life will stop, then we had best make haste to reduce our carbon footprint– not in order to be politically correct, but rather to strike a blow against the tyranny of the object. If we fear that, for purposes of GPS surveillance, we may one day be implanted with a microchip, then we had best soon rediscover how to come and go from our bodies. If Monsanto has insured the triumph of genetically modified Frankenfoods, then it might be best to think small; a few out-of-date seeds could be planted in the yard. Joyously simple, and on our backs carrying the sum of our experience, like the weight of the whole world, we must dare to be as naked as at the moment of our birth.

There is no door to the Macrocosm. Again, we must find the key.

Human Demonology

Salome

P. Emerson Williams

And when a convenient day was come, that Herod on his birthday made a supper to his lords, high captains, and chief estates of Galilee; And when the daughter of the said Herodias came in, and danced, and pleased Herod and them that sat with him, the king said unto the damsel, Ask of me whatsoever thou wilt, and I will give it thee. And he sware unto her, Whatsoever thou shalt ask of me, I will give it thee, unto the half of my kingdom. And she went forth, and said unto her mother, What shall I ask? And she said, The head of John the Baptist.

And she came in straightway with haste unto the king, and asked, saying, I will that thou give me by and by in a charger the head of John the Baptist. And the king was exceeding sorry; yet for his oath's sake, and for their sakes which sat with him, he would not reject her. And immediately the king sent an executioner, and commanded his head to be brought: and he went and beheaded him in the prison, and brought his head in a charger, and gave it to the damsel: and the damsel gave it to her mother. And when his disciples heard of it, they came and took up his corpse, and laid it in a tomb.

Mark 6:21-29, KJV

The story of Salome is a familiar one in Western culture, the climax of which with her lascivious dance and the severed head of John the Baptist has fired the imagination of artists, writers and composers for hundreds of years. Then there's Dracula as an allegory describing Victorian men's fear of female sexuality, Lilith in legend and art... The mythical Salome can be seen as both a product of and a window into the minds of those who told it. Salome was a real historical person, born EV 14, the daughter of Herodias and the stepdaughter of the Emperor Herod Antipas. Though she is unnamed in the New Testament, Salome is named in the writings of the historian Josephus.

There's a flavor to the tale that feels more like one from the old testament than the new. Her role in the book of Mark continues such tales of women and men's desire for them leading to degradation and murder as in the tale of Athaliah, who established the worship of the aggregate of all heathen gods Baal in Judah. Women are shown as leading men into sin from the very beginning with Eve, and before her, the lack of subservience in the uncontrollable Lilith has her cast out and transformed into a demon, stealing the children of Eve and seducing men in the night. Salome's actions combines the gruesomeness of the two mothers who, during the siege of King Ben-hadad in Samaria during a famine, conspired to boil the son of one to eat him with Jezebel, the proto-femme fatale, murderer, prostitute and enemy of God, though in her seduction of Herod, Salome is not leading a righteous man astray.

> No longer was she merely the dancing-girl who extorts a cry of lust and concupiscence from an old man by the lascivious contortions of her body; who breaks the will, masters the mind of a King by the spectacle of her quivering bosoms, heaving belly and tossing thighs; she was now revealed in a sense as the symbolic incarnation of world-old Vice, the goddess of immortal Hysteria, the Curse of Beauty supreme above all other beauties by the cataleptic spasm that stirs her flesh and steels her muscles, - a monstrous Beast of the Apocalypse, indifferent, irresponsible, insensible, poisoning.

J. K. Huysmans

It may be enlightening to consider whether the image of Herod lusting after his stepdaughter, is implied by he biblical text, (something not explicitly written), or if it is inferred by the reader. The only image more popular in the culture than Salome holding John the Baptist's head is her performing the erotically charged and iconic Dance of the Seven Veils. This dance originated in Oscar Wilde's play and later in Strauss' opera, and the first performances of the play was seen as outrageous at the time. In the popular imagination the players in this tale are demons in human form, but in the visions of artists, they are akin to the wrangling and screaming of gods. To see Wilde's play or Strauss' opera performed is like witnessing the machinations of Olympus. They occupy a dreamscape that is truly poetic in its decadence. And in what might be seen as the bizarro world equivalent, John the Baptist's severed head itself has been linked symbolically with the head of Baphomet that Templars were said to worship in their blasphemous rites.

> The representation of the egregore as bust recalls the ancient literary tradition of animated statues or Salome, who wanted the head of John the Baptist, probably to master his visionary powers.....The classic prototype of such an egregore is Baphomet, the alleged egregore of the Templars, who was (as the Roman Emperor of the Gods) likewise worshipped in the form of a bust. In the secret statutes of the Templars, Baphomet was besought with the introduction to the Qu'ran and dismissed with the 24th chapter of the Book of Sirach.

P. R. Koenig, from "Too Hot to Handle"

As for Salome holding and kissing the severed head, causing a shocked and disgusted Herod to order his soldiers to kill her, all historical accounts contradict this. In the writings of Josephus we find Salome marrying twice, giving birth several times and dying of old age. The image of Salome as a femme fatale can largely be traced back to Wilde's play and to the decadent artists if *fin de siecle* Vienna, at least in the popular mind, these creative minds didn't pull this out of their own minds fully formed. The historical facts about Salome (as far as we know them) differ from the legend in almost every detail and how the legend is what's known.

What is more interesting to me is how receptive the collective mind of Western culture was to the myth, and how it became a cultural touchstone at the time Bram Stoker tapped into the Victorian male's fear of female sexuality with Dracula. I would posit that Salome's tale as it evolved through the nineteenth century is a parable designed to convey that such a headstrong nature and unchecked sexuality in a woman of any age is a threat to the entire structure of society. The thread of stubborn, rebellious and non-conforming women in mythology and literature could have a link to how any behavior and sign of assertiveness on the part of the "second sex" can be linked to mental disorder and therefore "clinicized" and needing to be drugged into submission.

It is quite fitting that the tragic dream of Norma Desmond in Sunset Boulevard is to write and star in a film based on the story of Salome. The archetypal hero of film noir is on a runaway train to hell and disaster from the moment the femme fatale shows up.

We're pretty apocalyptically minded around these parts lately. Maybe that's because the personal, financial, national and international narrative right now looks like a bare-fisted steel cage death match between *1984* and *A Handmaid's Tale* over the battered corpse of *Brave New World*. We've found out the deceased didn't have enough insurance coverage to be kept alive for the sake of subduing independent thought and action among the populace of the developed world.

Vampire Sun, Werewolf Moon I

Wes Unruh

Two thousand years ago, today would have been the first day of Lupercalia.

Now bear with me, I haven't written like this in a while, but there is a link between Valentine's Day, the werewolf, Pan, and this piece which I'll explain in part 2. James' article on True Blood back in August of '09 convinced me to give that series a shot, and it's only fitting that this be the first post I publish on Modern Mythology, for reasons that I hope will become clearer as we continue.

In this piece I'll begin to highlight how the vampire manifests as an inversion of the solar hero and werewolf as inversion of the lunar hero's path. If you have seen contemporary texts like *Buffy*, *True Blood*, *Underworld*, *Supernatural*, or *Twilight* then you're more than empowered to know what I mean when I say vampire and werewolf.

While it seems that there are a lot of different ways that people manifest fantasy and fetish in their adult lives, fantasizing about vampires and werewolves is a consistent and resilient trend. More than enough ink has been devoted to why the vampire and the werewolf have continued to evolve alongside culture– and continue to also bring in revenue. With *Twilight*, vampires and werewolves created a high water mark in terms of pure profit for the publishing industry. Vampires and werewolves are the twin archetypal draws in western commercial pop culture.

The zombie comes in at a strong third, of course, especially when you lump in the promethean Frankenstien Monster– clearly a manifestation of fear of death combined with fear of eternity and given significant anchoring both in religious references and an entirely predictable fear of the exploited seeking vengeance. There's also the mind-controlled killer, a shadow of the zombified murderer most purely expressed in Fritz Lang's *The Cabinet of Dr. Caligari* and referenced nowadays as alternatively a "manchurian" / "monarch mind-control" assassin or as a shambling, brain-eating ghoul. I suspect there are far fewer teens laying awake at night longing to be turned into a mind-controlled killer or shambling, feral ghoul than there are teens hoping to be bitten by a werewolf or a vampire (although, if Poppy Z. Brite had written *Twilight*, perhaps things would be different.)

This hints at a kind of mythomathematics– there are certain innate qualities that dictate where vampire begins and ends, where werewolf begins and ends, and they both oppose and unite, a constant dance. The vampire is the inversion of the sun, specifically– not of light. The sun cannot see itself in the mirror, because it does nothing but radiate light– the vampire is the sun's shadow, and in it's presence ignites, becomes enflamed, and the vampire's individual self is eradicated.

The moon, however, is a reflective, mutable space– when the werewolf bathes in lunar light it changes, cycles. Why is the vampire destroyed by its symbol while the werewolf is transformed? It speaks to a larger mapping of symbol to myth.

The vampire is not a solar hero, it's an antithesis of that archetype– the solar hero is a conquering and vanquishing hero– so the vampire is changed, often destroyed utterly by the sun, and exists as the shadow of the sun. The werewolf, on the other hand, is lunar– the lunar hero does not conquer, the hero transforms, transcends, and overcomes through metamorphosis. The werewolf, on the other hand, is the inversion of the lunar hero– the werewolf is overcome by transformation when exposed to the full moon, and the transformation eradicates the consciousness, leaving only the Id behind and in charge.

Let me be clear, I do not think that writers sit down with a mythic map scripted, but rather that these mythic entities resonate in ways which lead the writer down culturally indicated paths. Stephanie Meyer distilled the essential duality then played within it as a melodramatic frame for teen angst. It is a formulae that produces catharsis and is obviously well-adapted to the present zeitgeist, much like J. K. Rowling's remarkable placement of Harry Potter into the vacuum left in culture by the evolution of Disney away from being the conduit by which magick and witchcraft could be safely sampled. Neither Meyer or Rowling are transgressing into the myth space– they are reinforcing it, and in many ways expanding it. Still the dualism of Sun and Moon remains strewn throughout the vampires and the werewolves of Stephanie Meyer, and the elite and the technologically enabled magical children, once almost entirely the dominion of Walt Disney's kingdom, are now flooding into the mindshare of the memeplex geographically materialized in the Wizarding World at Universal Orlando.

The sheer publishing glut of vampire and werewolf narratives ensures that every possible iteration of plot will eventually be explored, something that requires fan texts to enact this transgressive allegorythym. Transgressive Star Trek fan-fiction could assimilate the borg through some klingonicization into a functional part of the Federation– which to a Trekker is as queering of a social space as Harry/Draco fanfic is of a personal space to a young fan of Harry Potter.

Transgressive mythmaking becomes a space that calls to a writer because there a kind of synthesis can be achieved– transgressive art an inroad to synthesis– "Rejection" is a by-product of "acceptance" since it acknowledges existence, and allows the rejected a voice. Once the voice begins utterance, the possibility of a dialogue towards synthesis begins.

For a writer, there are a number of ways to play with transgression. *Blade*, for example, is an outsider, a queer in both vampire and human worlds, able to walk in sunlight. *Underworld* and its sequels all follow transgressive trends that seek a synthesis – as all thesis and antithesis must synthesize– and also in *Underworld* the vampire and werewolf trangressively merge into a queer razor-taloned green-skinned mutant who is both lunar and solar– conqueror of transformation.

Wes Unruh's previous writing appeared in several online publications, including an essay on bricolage, digital collage, and sigilization which appeared in Taylor Ellwood's *Manifesting Prosperity: A Wealth Magic* Anthology, and short fiction appearing in Twit Publishing Presents: *PULP!: Summer / Fall 2010 anthology*. Currently he is working on an alchemical adventure story entitled '*God Inc.*' and a longer work concerned with the future (or perhaps past) of humanity entitled *Memwar*.

Vampire Sun, Werewolf Moon II

Wes Unruh

It's VD day, which has come a long way since Lupercalia's formalized whipping ceremonies to make certain the women would be fertile for fall deliveries. Now VD means Valentine's Day, Venereal Disease, and Vampire Diaries, apparently concurrently if the commercials I saw during station breaks on Supernatural are any indication. Irreducible forms of sexual archetypal anxieties been with us forever–literally to pre-literate times and (as if as in a full eclipse) it has been overlayed by VD in the CW's programming. Here's the concise description given on Wikipedia of the Lupercalia:

> ...the Luperci cut thongs from the skins of the victims, which were called februa, dressed themselves in the skins of the sacrificed goats, in imitation of Lupercus, and ran round the walls of the old Palatine city, the line of which was marked with stones, with the thongs in their hands in two bands, striking the people who crowded near. Girls and young women would line up on their route to receive lashes from these whips. This was supposed to ensure fertility, prevent sterility in women and ease the pains of childbirth.

Who knows how long this had been going on; certainly as far back as the founding of Rome. This kept going until the vampire pope completely lost his shit and deliberately forced it to be enfolded into the purification of the Virgin aka Candlemas. Still, a good deal of the naked flogging is alive and well on V-Day if you go to the right shows. That aside, in part one I labeled vampires and werewolves as lunar and solar inversions of the hero.

Of course, labeling vampire solar and werewolf lunar then implies there are other planetary attributes which could manifest archetypes. One can find that the whole planetary array of these forms occurs in *Buffy*, *Supernatural*, and *True Blood*: fairies as Uranian, elves/aliens as Venusian, angelic or dragon forms as Mercurial, demonic or sadistic archetypes from Saturn, etc.– and while these other planetary presences are not always explicit, they are discursive gaps awaiting narration. However, barring the inner planets which perform slow, intricate dances across the night sky (if/when you can see the sky) the planets themselves are not nearly as visible as the sun and the moon– and likewise the impact of vampire and werewolf archetypes economically trumps all other mythic forms.

Secondly, at least as far as the werewolf is concerned, the linkage to the lunar cycle is a very modern invention. Frank Hamel's book *Human Animals*, published in 1915, relates a good number of "wer-wolf" tales from the past four hundred or so years and the moon is incidental. The first (and now lost) filmic portrayal of *The Werewolf* (1913) was more firmly rooted in colonialist fears of vengeance by witchcraft.

It wasn't until *Werewolf of London* (1935) that lunar light and werewolf bite came together to create the first filmic bipedal werewolf– all of the modern tropes of the werewolf were present. And this bipedal werewolf runs naked through the streets looking more like a man wearing goatskins than the traditional origins would have us believe. I'm making the case that Lupercalia is part of the essential mythic strand that generated the werewolf, even more-so than the lunar connection– that the full werewolf form of *Twilight's* wolves comes from a different folklore than the bipedal werewolf descended from ancient shepherds who were imitating Pan. The werewolf Lon Chaney portrays is almost identical to the *Teen Wolf* (1985) Michael J. Fox portrayed, a satyr more than a wolf, pure sexual Id run rampant upon transformation.

Now, just as the first filmic appearance of a werewolf's transformation is lost, so too is the first filmic appearance of Count Dracula in *Dracula's Death* (1923). I can't presume to know the elements in place in a lost film made in a language I don't speak, but in both *Nosferatu* (1922) and again explicitly with *Dracula* (1931) the vampire is clearly shown to be destroyed by sunlight– the vampire's position as an inversion of the solar hero seems always to be clear, it was for the 'children of the night' to be entrained into signifying the lunar, a position that didn't fully coalesce until Lon Chaney materialized them in *The Wolf Man* (1941) and its sequels. The first meeting of the werewolf and the vampire is in *House of Dracula* (1931) and it is on this tenuous strand that countless reoccurring forms continue to overlap.

But perhaps there's something more going on underneath– this solar, lunar inversion is a clue– the vampire and the werewolf come from the same space, a shadowy understanding of superstitions and an overlay on demonized and outmoded beliefs. It is a long way from *House of Dracula* to *True Blood*, both in terms of geographic setting and temporal space, but also in terms of how the idea of the world these entities require to exist has evolved. In *True Blood*, the vampire elite rule through an elaborate global empire, a regime based on bloodlines, secret allegiances, and brutal violence carried out by vampire assassins and the occasional pack of Nazi werewolf henchmen. Unpacking all the new mythographic materials layered into the last few seasons of *True Blood* will keep some lucky television-studies scholar occupied for the next decade. Clearly these build atop a house of cards that wouldn't stand without much of the media-mythic content the preceded it, whether a foundation build in pop culture awareness by Stoker's *Dracula* or Rice's *Interview With A Vampire* or even White Wolf's World of Darkness RPG.

Where there is an empire, there are the voiceless and often faceless victims of power. Especially in *True Blood* both vampire and werewolf elite are able to murder with impunity, protected by the invisible empire. In *Blade II* the vampire elite control the world in ways that go far beyond that, where farming blood is true industrial production. This is a far cry from the fate of the *Werewolf of London*, as a sole victim murdered was enough to unwind the sole villain into an act of suicidal self-sabotage.

Now the normalized narratives are strewn through with the unacknowledged / unacknowledgeable, there only to be consumed in service to the true rulers of the regime. Constantly the theme in these inverted archetypal tropes is one of social acknowledgment– either as a lover or acknowledgment of hunger– here vampire treads close to zombie perhaps, the starved vampire, strung-out and scrambling through sewers like del Toro's vision in Blade II, contrast the vampire Illuminati bloodlines that orchestrate a vast world government behind the scenes. These archetypal signifiers now carry so much cultural currency that they appeal to the weakest, who see themselves as that nameless, voiceless victim, and long to be the empowered.

Co-Operate or Die

James Curcio

I posted the following recently, and it got a fair amount of thumbs-up around the fishbowl:

The myth of "everyone for themselves" will get you killed in the years that are coming. Learn to work together and be committed to your team. Corporations, major political groups give us no umbrage, so fuck them. Find trustworthy people. Be trustworthy. That's all I've got.

I'd like to explain what I meant a little more, but first I need to take a step back.

As we have explored here, as well in *The Immanence of Myth*: we live by our myths. They compound one upon the other, build up, not so much in direct hierarchies as in striated patterns. They are chaotic, intertwined and tangled, and can be hard to look at one at a time.

Still, we try.

There is one that has been especially present to my mind of late. This is the idea of "everyone for themselves," as it contrasts myths of cooperation. This myth is popular in America. It helps support the idea that the poor deserve to be poor, that they are simply lazy, and that the rich are inherently superior. This myth is also connected to "pulling ourselves up by our bootstraps," the objectivist self-determination of Rand, the separation of bodies and minds, and to hell with government oversight and regulations, rigged but ostensibly "free" markets will sort themselves out.

You see how these myths tangle into each other, like a pile of ¼" cables left in a studio closet too long. You may find yourself feeling very strongly that the government should keep out of our lives, and at the same time believe in cooperation as central to survival, over and above competition. We contradict ourselves. We contradict one another, and we mean different things when we use the same words. This part of the discussion could take me far afield of what I actually want to explore, but I hope you can see my point without devolving into the party-line arguments between Democrat and Socialist, Republican and Libertarian. I have no political agenda, only a humanitarian one.

Instead, read this Wiki article if you'd rather see where I'm going with this, but remember what I said: myths are not just theoretical. Because these myths are not abstract theories, they determine how we treat one another, how we behave, how we live. What we value.

When Richard Dawkins set out to "examine the biology of selfishness and altruism" in The Selfish Gene, *he reinterpreted the basis of evolution, and therefore of altruism. He was "not advocating a morality based on evolution", and even felt that "we must teach our children altruism, for we cannot expect it to be part of their biological nature." But John Maynard Smith was showing that behavior could be subject to evolution, Robert Trivers had shown that reciprocal altruism is strongly favored by natural selection to lead to complex systems of altruistic behavior (supporting Kropotkin's argument that cooperation is as much a factor of evolution as competition), and Axelrod's dramatic results showed that in a very simple game the conditions for survival (be "nice", be provocable, promote the mutual interest) seem to be the essence of morality. While this does not yet amount to a science of morality, the game theoretic approach has clarified the conditions required for the evolution and persistence of cooperation, and shown how Darwinian natural selection can lead to complex behavior, including notions of morality, fairness, and justice. It is shown that the nature of self-interest is more profound than previously considered, and that behavior that seems altruistic may, in a broader view, be individually beneficial. Extensions of this work to morality and the social contract may yet resolve the old issue of individual interests versus group interests.*

Cooperation functions just fine when it is personally motivated, but this does not mean that putting the group above ones self in certain cases *is not* of greater long-term benefit.

When we live by the myth of "everyone for themselves," in a society that supports this belief, we feel self-entitled when we do well, and we feel guilty when we do not. It was, in this mindset, strictly our fault if we didn't succeed by our rules, and maybe if we just thought more positively it would all get better. The whole world rests on our shoulders. This attitude also is a logical cultural conclusion to the Enlightenment project.

Contrary to the myth that many of the wealthy have some unique skill or power, it has been documented that, for instance, professional investors barely outperform the random results. As economist Burton Malkiel said, "a blindfolded monkey throwing darts at a newspaper's financial pages could select a portfolio that would do just as well as one carefully selected by experts." In fact, in some tests of this concept, they have underperformed it. (Look at the fourteen year long analysis performed by the Wall Street Journal on the subject.)

Though traits like persistence certainly can't hurt, "success" is not ensured through any particular deed, nor failure by a particular misdeed. In other words, the poor don't "deserve" to be poor any more than the rich "deserve" to be rich, myths of entitlement notwithstanding. That's just how things have turned out for the moment.

As I look around me and see friends and acquaintances lose jobs, go unemployed for long periods, lose their homes, drop off the grid altogether, I also see groups of us attempting to band together, dropping the "Jersey Shore bullshit," and helping each other. Whatever it takes to help each other survive and succeed. I too have been struggling– not to keep productive, that has never been hard for me– but to find a way of monetizing all the values I produce which seem to almost be in direct contradiction to the "values" espoused by hard-line capitalism. And I have found that the only way I am going to survive is by finding people that I can count on, and through people maximizing one another's strengths and mutually minimizing our weaknesses.

It's easy to make this sound like theory. I've been talking about this for years now, with friends and collaborators, and have seen "test groups" (if you want to call it that) splinter and fall apart because there wasn't enough external conflict to distract from the production of internal conflict. I've seen many of them fail because none of us have been trained to work well together. We've only been taught how to work for ourselves and to compete. And many of our myths do not support true cooperation and support.

When there is an identified "external threat" it is easier for people to band together against that threat, to feel a common bond, to identify and align their behavior through mutually beneficial patterns because the alternative is anathema to self preservation. I imagine it was the binding glue of Feudalism. So, without that, groups often degenerate into as I've called "Jersey Shore bullshit." Even when the people involved are otherwise smart. Then it just becomes *pedantic* Jersey Shore bullshit.

From the perspective of narrative, all drama is conflict, and you can't have a story without drama. But in terms of our lives, in theory, many of us would probably like to mitigate conflict as much as possible. Many people manufacture conflict in the form of drama when natural conflict doesn't already arise. I think this is something that can be undone, I don't think it *has* to be that way, but I've seen it plenty. Bored people have so much drama in their lives, even if precious little genuine conflict. So– as the famous Chinese curse says– may you live in interesting times.

We've always known that narrative depends on conflict. You can't tell a story without an internal or external conflict. Maybe it isn't only true in fiction. Maybe we do thrive on conflict.

I think– I hope I'm wrong– that class stratification, tensions from increasing pressures driven by corporate owned resources, etc in coming decades *invariably* leads to a place where the disenfranchised, otherwise well-intentioned individual can't help but become some form of *outlaw*. "We" need cells, safe-houses, methods for the production and securing of goods, value to some extent excluded from corporate control. This is an incredible undertaking, one which most of us are in no way prepared for. But parenthood is also a tremendous undertaking which most are not prepared for. We may have to learn as we go or die trying.

To go beyond that point, we need to ask, in what can "we" be constructed without re-capitulating the Us / Them process? This posture is biologically conditioned, but biology itself is not entirely immutable.

Unicellular to multi-cellular evolution took a seemingly inordinate amount of time, that is, until you consider the systemic leap that is required between a single unit, with a single will, and multiple units with a shared will. (Though it's worth mentioning that even unicellular organisms seem to communicate via a chemical language.) This complexity certainly shouldn't be lost on anyone who has tried to make a decision when in a group, and how the layers of expectation and posturing, demand and avoidance, can compound until it is quite simply impossible for the group-as-such to make a decision at all, and it invariably fragments in any number of ways. In layman's terms, democracy is slow and often irritating.

This is problematic not just in the most obvious sense– in the sense in which any being that *thinks of itself as having a singular will* – must attempt to couple that with an overarching group objective. "Agreement" so often demands compromise, conquest, even genocide; conflict is the result not necessarily of flaw, but rather an abundance of divergent wills. The natural world is rife with conflict and fecund birth-conflict-consumption-death for this very reason. Life has always been "against all odds," not an agreement met and reached through parliamentary debate.

It seems almost impossible to avoid an entropic movement toward one of several equally undesirable states in one way or another: fascism, where all individual wills are relegated to the group will, which itself will invariably be co-opted by a singular will, or destabilization, where energy is fed endlessly in the system until it eventually, necessarily, must dissolve, most likely to the mutual disappointment of those involved. This is especially problematic for utopian models, but it is equally problematic for the transition from essential (theoretical) to functional democracy. Put one hundred people in a room, give them a system that forces true egalitarianism, and try to get them to reach a consensus about what to have for lunch and you'll quickly see the problem here.

Political problems are thus social problems, and social problems are thus personal, if we open the supposed "singularity" of ourself as organism into the chaotic array of different bodies that it actually is. The singularity is one myth, an equally viable one is that "we" are legion. This demands a recognition of systemic factors rather than a personal evaluation, and it is because of this that observations garnered from one scale–the biological interaction of "harmful" and "helpful" bacteria within "our" bodies, all so defined from the perspective of the will that defines itself–might be applicable to another, even if some assumption of scalability may be specious or even in error. (For instance, the analysis of matter at quantum and relativistic scales.)

This is probably a simplification of several Deleuze and De Landa's ideas, though I hope even sketches in this direction will be a little more accessible to the general reader than *1000 Plateaus.*

Be that as it may, I'd like to present the thought that a consideration of the means by which cells co-operate by design might be studied with the intent of modeling for social and political ends, as we see the political structures in place, all based on ideals grounded in the long-failed Enlightenment Agenda, tremble and buckle the world over.

Let me be honest, though. I'm dubious of any political system either a) functioning the way it is designed to function or b) being in the best interest of the majority of the public once the game has been set in motion and left to run for a mere century or two. Quite possibly the only way this could come about is if the world population (of humans) was considerably lower than it is. I f we're going to see a return to tribalism in some sense as a survival technique– as it's always been for humans– I don't know about you, but I want an intentional family I can trust. We have to drop the "everyone for themselves" bullshit to the extent that we realize that our best chances of survival are *not* alone. Humans have always banded together to survive.

To reiterate what I said: *be trustworthy. Find those you can trust. That's all I've got.*

The Myth of Work vs The Reality of Abuse

James Curcio

I'd like to touch on yet another issue which, frankly, could be the topic of a book unto itself. And it's a book that, if it hasn't been written already, should be written. It needs to be written, and more importantly, it needs to be talked about.

Every culture has myths about work. What is acceptable for an employee or employer, what the nature of that relationship should be. It is in the benefit of the employer to have myths throughout the workforce that tie their very identity and sense of self worth into how well they meet that employers demands, and if there aren't forces in place, either enforced through government oversight or the unionization of the workers in some configuration, these myths can run rampant. There is, after all, a word in Japanese for working one's self to death. (They also apparently have a word for eating one's self to ruin. But that's another story.)

None of these myths are inherently good or bad. They simply render a psychological and then material result, which we might be prone to evaluate ethically.

Elements of our religions provide the infrastructure for these myths. They are further re-enforced by our social institutions, our education in many cases being little more than a tool for shaping people into effective workers as defined by the mandates of society.

This process is not inherently good or bad. As I said in the chapter on initiation in *The Immanence of Myth*, the prescriptive nature of indoctrination may sound ominous, but many of us know what humans become when left to be feral creatures. They can hardly be called human, at all.

However, this process can still break down in any number of ways. And I believe many of you will agree, it is breaking down in a fundamental way in the United States, and it is getting worse.

There was an article in Mother Jones entitled "All Work And No Pay" that I suggest you read immediately. I will include only a short excerpt,

... now we no longer even acknowledge it– not in blue-collar work, not in white-collar or pink-collar work, not in economics texts, and certainly not in the media (except when journalists gripe about the staff-compacted-job-expanded newsroom). Now the word we use is "productivity," a term insidious in both its usage and creep. The not-so-subtle implication is always: Don't you want to be a productive member of society? Pundits across the political spectrum revel in the fact that US productivity (a.k.a. economic output per hour worked) consistently leads the world. Yes, year after year, Americans wring even more value out of each minute on the job than we did the year before. U-S-A! U-S-A!

Except what's good for American business isn't necessarily good for Americans. We're not just working smarter, but harder. And harder. And harder, to the point where the driver is no longer American industriousness, but something much more predatory.

The analogy made in this article to an abusive relationship is spot on. When one partner has no income, and the other does, and the rich one is punching the other in the face over and again, do we tell them to stick around because, "how will you afford to live"?

If so, we've just bought into a culture of abuse.

And many of us are so used to this state of affairs that not only does it seem normal, but we actually find ourselves sticking up for the bully. In fact, I would say that the majority of the Tea Party is founded on the psychology of Stockholm Syndrome.

It is not insane to demand that employers provide livable wages and treat their workers– all of them– as human beings. With respect and dignity. I will not hear any whining about how it's too expensive. If it is too expensive within the present system to maintain a workforce that is treated humanely, who are entrusted to embody the values that the company pretends to espouse, then the system itself needs to be dismantled. By the hands of the workers, if need be.

Each of us has a breaking point, and it is different for each of us. I don't know what yours is, and it isn't my place to say. But if you feel you are being pushed up to it and beyond over and again, and you're stomaching it out of fear, out of the belief that it's normal to feel this way: open your eyes. It isn't normal, it's an abusive relationship. And it should be treated like any other abusive relationship. Stop making excuses for your abuser, and get the fuck out.

If that doesn't seem like an option to you because you can't figure out how you'll afford to live without it, that is exactly the thinking they're counting on. I was once given a piece of advice that has always stuck with me: *never take a meeting that you can't walk away from.*

Pesky things like love and responsibility to the people that we love often sidelines such samurai-like dedication to ideals. If you have a child to care for, an out-of-work spouse, etc, then you may well feel up against the wall if you're working a job that treats you like a subhuman and pays you table scraps. Like many Americans in the past, if you walk this path, you may discover a subconscious resentment building over the decades as the awful jobs thanklessly break you down, and you find yourself coming to hate all that you'd loved. Drink enough, let the hate fly, and soon you've joined in on the circle of abuse.

So, don't be a part of that statistic if you can help it. Like I said, we all know our breaking point, and we all know how to soldier well past it. Don't. If, on other hand, you're nowhere near it, then consider yourself lucky and be on your merry way.

I don't have an easy solution to any of this. No one does. If we did, I would sure as hell hope that we wouldn't be such a self-abusive race. I do know that I'm willing to die for my convictions if need be. (Though like anyone else, I'd rather not.) What about you?

And please, don't try to read through this that I'm advocating the dissolution of work, that I'm advocating laziness. I'm simply advocating a return to sanity. Though on that note, we may want to consider this, from an article Rushoff ran on CNN entitled "Are Jobs Obsolete?"

> We're living in an economy where productivity is no longer the goal, employment is. That's because, on a very fundamental level, we have pretty much everything we need. America is productive enough that it could probably shelter, feed, educate, and even provide health care for its entire population with just a fraction of us actually working.
>
> According to the U.N. Food and Agriculture Organization, there is enough food produced to provide everyone in the world with 2,720 kilocalories per person per day. And that's even after America disposes of thousands of tons of crop and dairy just to keep market prices high. Meanwhile, American banks overloaded with foreclosed properties are demolishing vacant dwellings to get the empty houses off their books.
>
> Our problem is not that we don't have enough stuff—it's that we don't have enough ways for people to work and prove that they deserve this stuff.

Myth As A Weapon

Doctor Adventure!

What would you do if you walked outside one day and saw something you *knew* with absolute certainty was imaginary? Something impossible. Would you cry with sadness or delight? Would you scream, or run, or fight? Would you make friends?

Every-day the world is getting stranger. The rules we have been taught govern reality and life and circumstance have long fallen, useless and wheezing, to the ground. Fuck knows if I've been alive before, but I'm here *now* and this place is *weird*! I wouldn't have it any other way, really.

As the yarn begins to unravel– "as the sheep is sheared" may be more appropriate – the various social, economic, political, educational, emotional, psychological, physical and spiritual frameworks that have up 'till now defined our existence are dissolving. Due to an odd quirk of the human cognitive apparatus (wink wink) this phenomenon also has certain quantum level repercussions that might destabilize your local reality. FUCK! (If you don't believe me, ask a physicist that isn't a chicken-shit.)

And here we stand, on the edge of this wild future, with the Towers crumbling, the robots taking up arms, prehistoric toxic ooze poisoning the ocean not to mention swirling garbage islands, and Godzilla rising from slumber. Figuratively, at the very least.

Can you look me in the eye and tell me these things can be handled using "conventional" means? Playing it safe? No. You'd be a goddamned liar. Humanity has used the subterfuge of conventionality, re-enforced ignorance to disguise the fact that most of the people in charge haven't a fucking *clue* what should actually be done to make the world a better place. Which is fine, they've been consumed by their own machine, and it has defined their limitations. The machine, however, lives in the real world, the one carved in stone and blood. They, often, do not.

If the drive to be legendary is innate, then the mass hysteria caused by the pressure of denying it makes a lot of the turmoil in the world suddenly make sense. As usual, humanity has been playing in God's toolshed without reading any of the instructions.

(Like giving a shotgun to a pissed-off blindfolded 6 year old on too much soda and Adderall. Bad news all around.)

Still, these bumbling attempts to make the world better have yielded strange fruit: entities and mechanisms of a titanic and horrific scale. Corporate egragores. They ate their creators long ago.

But what about those that have always peeked behind the curtain? Throughout human history there have been stories about people that were *more* than people. Some stories say they're on their way, others that they left long ago, and some very popular ones about their return. These stories emerge in times of struggle.

Forged like diamonds under the stress, from these myriad and tremendous pressures are heroes and legends distilled. Like I said before though, this place is WEIRD! The tools we have to reshape our perceptions are powerful, prevalent and cheap. The tools we have to reshape the world around us are staggering in their scope and precision. What happens when you throw THAT into the mix? All of a sudden you've got real live mythic super-people running amok on a planet where most folks are living in a

goddamn video game and shitting themselves in terror at whatever fear porn the cook up on TV.

I'm talking the whole nine yards by the way; trip-headed telekinetic Bodhisattvas, Super-Heroes and Villains, trans-dimensional hyper intelligences, cyborg call-girls, mutants, ancient monsters and the undead. Scary as it is, they're humanities only hope at not completely and utterly fucking themselves into oblivion.

Also, far as I can tell, they're *us*. Us. You and me.

We stand poised and ready to strike at the heart of the Beast with weapons forged from science and art, ancient magic, hardcore hyper-space drugs and the heat from the heart of the sun. But, are we starting a fight or playing a game?

If you haven't noticed, I'm not talking about protest or war. I'm talking about solving the problems that need to be dealt with, setting an example on a grand scale and providing working alternatives. The hard part of course is how the hell do you figure these things out?

We play.

The inherent biological mechanism for discovery and expression is *play*.

Play is as serious as life and death. We are made of dreams. Play teaches us what we are, what we could be and how the fuck to get there. Making a game that everyone can take part in is the trick, and always remember that the rules are just there to make things more interesting.

We are the players– the cast and crew. We set the stage, prepare our roles, build the props, paint the sets and become the Story.

Go do something impossible. Now.

Welcome to the *Future*!

Transmedia mythology

James Curcio

In the closing section of this book, before we present some conversations, I'd like to look at issues pertaining to media and the production of media within the framework we have laid out.

So I'd like to cut to one of the buzz-words in production right now: transmedia.

Haven't heard it? Well, there has been. I swear.

Transmedia is the technique of telling stories across multiple platforms and formats using current digital technologies.

Heaven knows there are, quite suddenly, a lot of transmedia evangelists out there. So I just want to talk over some of the possibilities presented by transmedia storytelling as a concept, without pretending that this is the final word on anything.

Most of us (er, them) are motivated by deep excitement. And of course, many corporations are also excited by it as a new way of perceiving the "life cycle of their brands," and "customer engagement," and other terms that sound really creepy in the "bad touch" kind of way. But we see all of the possibilities for new ways of engaging with content. Some of us see exciting creative possibilities and some see dollar signs. (I prefer to see both, when possible.)

Engagement. Right there, some people get lost. "You mean there is more than one *way* to engage with content?"

Yes, there is. It is not just that you *are* engaged, but also *how*.

Let's consider a few of the ways that we take in media.

When you read a book, you're engaging with that story in a very different way then when it is shown to you in a comic, and when you watch a movie. Your brain is being engaged in different ways to create the narrative. It happens in you, after all, not on the screen or book.

With a comic book, you are imagining the continuity of time, you are building mental movies out of the storyboard of the comic. The artist provides static visual cues.

With a book, you are given the conceptual cues, but all of the sense experience has to be engaged. As such, it is both deeply rewarding, because so much of the creative process is left up to you, and very difficult in terms of generating engagement, because it isn't a passive process.

With a novel, there is a high entrance price, and a potentially big payoff. Movies are a passive process where visual, temporal, auditory cues are provided. Boredom is a potential enemy in all cases, but since there's a larger investment in reading a book, it seems to follow that if you get more than halfway through a book, you've already invested so much in creating that experience that you will insist on seeing it through to the end. It's very easy to switch channels on the TV, or surf away through YouTube or Netflix. Commitment seems to be so low on a platform like YouTube that it can be hard to keep attention for as "much" as two minutes.

Let's think on this for a moment before moving on to transmedia. Tell me if you have heard any statements like these lately:

"I used to read a lot, but I don't anymore really."

"I just can't seem to focus enough to read these days."

"I don't enjoy reading. I do too much of it on the computer at work as it is."

And so on. I hear these as reasons why people don't read any books at all. My emotional response is somewhere between sadness and abject terror. If this is as much of an epidemic as it seems to be from the people I talk to, then we have a serious issue on our hands.

Books are like maps to mental or emotional territories. We've still got to go *there* ourselves. From a lot of reviews that I read, I mean of other people's books, I feel like more and more readers expect a book to somehow reach out and knock them over the head the way a $100 million tent-pole Hollywood movie can.

In other words, people have become so used to what I would call exclusively passive entrainment, that they no longer have derive pleasure from the additional effort that is required for active entrainment. When you read a book, it is triggering your imagination. The book is merely a guide, but it is coming to life inside of you. In fact, many times when people find a failing in a book, it is a failing in themselves. (Though certainly there are many ways that an author can fail their audience. Many, many ways. But if someone can't stand Jazz, even Coltrane is just blowing in the wind.)

I offer you a challenge, if you are one of the people who has been making statements like the ones I began with: for one month, I challenge you to make yourself read for one hour, every day. That's it. One hour, every day. Could be on the bus. Could be at home. But do it at a time when you still have the mental energy to breathe life into what you are reading, because, remember, unlike the television or movie screen, a book depends almost entirely on you. It's quite a responsibility, and an interesting relationship, shared in silence between author and reader.

If after a month nothing has caught your attention, I don't know, man. Maybe you're a goner. (There's absolutely nothing wrong in my opinion with taking in narrative content from a screen. Some "readers" like to look down their nose, as if every episodic series is the intellectual and moral equivalent of *Full House*, and every movie is *Snakes On A Plane*. No. There is just something different about reading a book. Do both.)

It stands to reason that regardless of format, all of these are blueprints for an experience.

Of course, there's a dark potential in transmedia that the conspiracy theorists have also latched onto, producing a sort of paranoid PR-wing to the transmedia movement. I can't say if this paranoia is well placed or not, because it is based around things that haven't happened yet. (Maybe.) Can't see the ominous implication of transmedia? The fears engaged here are what drive the plot of the movie, *The Game*.

Namely, if transmedia is a way of telling related narratives across multiple mediums, it becomes increasingly immersive for an audience that invests the energy to read a book, watch a movie, and even interact with the characters in the story and one another within the context or the narrative.

As a creative obsessive, I see this as a good thing. And I see projects experimenting with the possibilities. For example:

> *CFG is a participatory drama that will play out this summer, with a cast of more than 400 spread over five countries. The plot centres around a secret society whose aim is to change the world; the society has decided to go public and CFG is the recruitment campaign. The narrative will be played out over web videos, interactive puzzles (including clues hidden inside real MP3s such as tracks on the White Album by The Beatles), mobile apps and real-life events. The project is sponsored by Nokia, and a website went live on May 17. This features a video from Tim Kring, who asks visitors to participate in a movement to drive real-world change through interactive storytelling.*
>
> *The creative team at The company P, Sandberg's transmedia production business, staged several tests last winter and spring. The Stockholm event ironed out kinks in the mobile technology used. More importantly, it honed the team's storytelling. "We learned how to spread people out so as to have the sense of being at the mercy of a big adventure."* **Wired.**

Let's look at function rather than form. The media we have at our disposal are partially new, social media especially, but "transmedia" presents an entire *mythological pantheon*, rather than a singular myth, as you might have within a single book or book series.

This approach would lend us toward long-running projects, projects that can span entire careers, where each item is unique and essentially stand alone, but mythically related to the others.

If you look at the long-running history of Christianity, Hinduism, Buddhism, or any other religion, you see a *multi-generational transmedia story* in effect. Many of those stories have real flesh and blood body counts. That's the side of transmedia that is troubling to most, where we become so immersed in our stories that we kill one another for them.

Whatever term we use– "transmedia" is a fine one, don't get me wrong– it is most important from here to look forward and ask "how can these tools be used to produce something beneficial to ourselves and the world?"

That is all of our task. I challenge you, dare you, *beg* you to do better than I have and will. And I'll feel no worse off for it, because our only true competitor is ourselves. But if it helps you get off your ass if I throw down the silk hanker-chef, well. I just did.

What Exactly is Transmedia Storytelling?

(And Does it Even Matter?)

Gunther Sonnenfeld

Good stories are timeless.

So why is it that we are often confined by media constructs, such as campaigns, which have specific in-points and end-points in time?

Why is it that we gravitate to buzzwords, and supersede powerful, emergent disciplines (such as transmedia storytelling) with notions of the "way things have to be" given these formative points in time?

Over time, we've argued over story. We've argued about stories. We've challenged our beliefs in them– just look at history. And over time, we've developed a sense of narrative by virtue of the channels we've created. Yet, ironically, we are bound to those channels by way of media and technology, and to a lesser extent, *context*. We always have been.

If we can look at time as simply the *measurement of intervals between events*, its relegation to manufactured thinking, or its basis in historical relevance, this was the initial impetus for what has evolved as *transmedia storytelling*.

As with anything cool and unique, the notion of "transmedia" tends to be adopted in phenomenon and language, and often misused or misunderstood. Banish or change the term if you like, I don't really care.

As a creative media and technology misfit of sorts, I've written quite a lot about "it" and spoken about "it" and actually practice "it" more out of a fascination with this notion of "transcendent media," not so much as a discipline that can be broken down into best practices or methodologies and even frameworks that can be serialized, but rather one that can't. The beauty of what have been determined to be transmedia vehicles or platforms is that *they are wonderfully unpredictable, reflexive, imaginative and kinetic*.

I won't distill the point by generating a list of "transmedia examples", nor will I go on a rant about how the various media markets are dying their own deaths. This is fairly obvious if you pay attention to what's being thrown at you everyday in the way of messaging and God only knows what else.

Quite simply, I gravitated to "transmedia storytelling" because it gave me an opportunity to liberate my ideas, and explore a *narrative interdependency (versus a codependency) between technology and media, and more importantly, between people.*

This doesn't make me a subject matter expert, or a guru, or a futurist, or someone assigned to any other ridiculous designation. But I am, and I am proud to say, that I am a practitioner. To borrow from the great William Goldman, *no one really knows anything.* Be that as it may, I am *student like all of you* who can share his knowledge and experience in the pursuit of higher learning and collective intelligence. The confidence I have in my own opinion is born out of this *determination.*

As with anything we've done or anything we do in technology and media, the tendency is to align ourselves with a clique of one type or another. I don't care what side or channel you're in or on, what matters is that you can appeal to the best and the most curious in human behavior, and that you can use technology and media for what they can be... Platforms that can help us transcend our more traditional thinking.

Furthermore, whatever we choose to call "it", "it" should not only influence behavior, but *endeavor to change behavior.*

A good number of folks who have helped pioneer or develop "transmedia" in various ways– people like Jeff Gomez, Stephen Dinehart, Christy Dena, Lina Srivastava, Mike Monello, Nedra Weinrich, Scott Walker, Robert Pratten and Ivan Askwith– will all tell you that "it" has this power. And power, of course, is something that we already possess, it just needs to be cultivated in ways that are meaningful.

In other words, once we can get over our technology and media hubris, *the real work has yet to be done.*

So, I don't think it's really a matter of what transmedia *is,* what it has *done,* or necessarily what it *does* in the context of now, but rather what it *represents.* Which is, quite simply, *possibility.*

Now, to get a bit more specific (and a bit less lofty), I think it is important to make a significant distinction between *technological* and *cultural disruption.*

Fact is, technology will continue to evolve, but the real evolution culminates in the iterative cycles we undergo in our relationship to narrative. *Story has an undeniable and somewhat impermeable place in our own genealogy,* and I think the more obvious manifestation of this resides in historical debate, and the less obvious dynamic resides in our attraction to fiction. Clearly, what has given rise to the narrative adoption of fantasy elements (such as comic books) is a relatedness to things that are a part of our own history, and most likely things about our history that we cannot comprehend, yet things that define us quite formatively as human beings. This seems fascinating.

If we can accept *story as genealogy* as a precept of our faith in the unknown, and an opportunity to *transcend through media,* then we have something very special that we can call our own. And, as we are discovering more and more, we can cultivate it through networks of people.

Where does technology (ala platform) then play a vital role? In *audience delivery* and *participatory appeal*.

Here's what I mean.

Aside from the narrative prospects, I believe that most media companies (and by "media" I mean any entity that produces andor distributes content) fail to understand that convergence is a matter of understanding and extracting the anthropological elements of participation, from ontologies to folksonomies to emotional mapping and geo-spatial integrations.

Further, things like AR, ARG and LARP extensions provide new perspectives on the realities we already share. To put it more simply, what we share in the way of context, consensus and relatedness is precisely what makes our media more sustainable, our products and services more resonant, and our identities more powerful.

This, in my humble opinion, is the true value of what transmedia storytelling can afford us: *the ability to synthesize narrative and platform in ways that are self-revealing, regenerative, altruistic, and ultimately, scalable.*

This is why gameplay can be so appealing: it allows us to collectively (and individually) explore our notions of *what we value*, whether we are duly cognizant of them or not. The point is not so much if games can change the way we look at the world, rather how we look at the world when we play them. Big difference.

We can also ascribe *sentient and empathic value* to gameplay, but that of course depends on the types of games we choose to play. Or does it?

Winning a game is a subjective experience. (Faulkner would argue that the battle only reveals to man his own folly...). If we liken this to the challenges we face with media in general, we can come to the quick realization that we must make our own meaning. However, if we can deliver audiences to brands, and audiences to other audiences, which we can, the sky really is the limit as to what is *transformative* with respect to our consumption.

Then, maybe, we no longer consume: we co-create, we co-own and we share.

But of course, we have the old media mavens to contend with - the gatekeepers that are stuck on controlling the gateways, as opposed to liberating them, despite the fact that transmedia vehicles provide more opportunity to actually sell more media.

Then again, what does "selling more media" do for us anyway?

Put it this way: *we've commercialized our ideas for centuries, why not break the patterns that clearly don't work?*

So, perhaps it's time we stopped bickering over name and process, and put our intentions to good use. Again, the real work has yet to be done.

In **Gunther Sonenfeld's** creative past, he won top honors at X-Dance for my work on the documentary "FLOW." Presently, he is a transmedia designer on "Algren," a cross-platform narrative of Nelson Algren's influence on prolific artists such as Lou Reed, Johnny Depp, David Mamet, Russell Banks and Michael Mann. Additionally, he is co-developing an educational ARG called "Gates of the West" that puts players into different scenarios within modern history.

He has keynoted alongside the likes of Sir Richard Branson, Mitch Joel, Arianna Huffington, Jonathan Harris and Jeffrey Hayzlett, and is working on his second book entitled "A Literacy of the Imagination," an exploration of the new storytelling paradigm and its influence in shaping the collaborative economy.

Questions towards a Philosophy of Gaming

Transmedia, and Myth

James Curcio

Within three hours of the 9/11 attacks on the Pentagon and the World Trade Center, a primarily American group of online gamers known as the Cloudmakers had gathered in their usual forum, a public message board. Their discussions began, like so many others around the world, with reactions of shock, prayers, and speculation. By the day's end, however, the tenor of the Cloudmakers' conversations had shifted dramatically. In sharp contrast to the feelings of confusion, fear, and powerlessness that seemed to overwhelm public and private discourse in America during the first 24 hours after the attacks, many of the Cloudmakers' (then) 7332 members began advocating a startlingly confident and organized response to the threat and mystery posed by the day's events. Posts with subjects like "The Darkest Puzzle" and "Cloudmakers to the Rescue!" argued passionately that a game-play mindset was, for them, an appropriate and productive way to confront the stark reality of 9/11.

"We can solve the puzzle of who the terrorists are," one member wrote. Another agreed: "We have the means, resources, and experience to put a picture together from a vast wealth of knowledge and personal intuition."

One Cloudmaker suggested:

"Let's become a resource. Utilize your computer & analytical talents to generate leads." Someone else implored: "We like to flout [sic] our 7,000 members and our voracious appetite for difficult problems, but when the chips are down can we really make a difference?" The Cloudmakers, who proudly identified themselves in member profiles, home pages and email signatures as "a collective intelligence unparalleled in entertainment history," were on the case– a very real case– despite the fact that their previous problem-solving experience as a group was limited solely to the virtual puzzles of a wholly fictional, massively multiplayer Web game known as "the Beast." (**"This Is Not a Game: Immersive Aesthetics and Collective Play," McGonigal.**)

There is a clear connection between games, gaming, and myth.

However, the layers of this connection cut much deeper than surface analogies. I'd like to look at the process of analysis, or de-construction, that many of the writers in this book have been taking. This is a "tip of the iceberg," type of inquiry, which is to say that my goal is to formulate the question throughout this article, without focusing on answers. That comes next, and is for people who are actually working in gaming. Maybe with you.

The most common form of analysis is simple correspondence. This is the layer of looking at something– let's say a specific game, like *Final Fantasy VII* and then making an association, such as "look at how this other specific myth was an influence on the game," Intentionally or unintentionally. For instance, the villain is named Sephiroth. So someone might, by way of a minor revelation or simple distraction, make an inference about an underlying Qabbalistic theme in the game. What does that do for us? Most college papers work like this: relate Charles Dickens' *Tale of Two Cities* to Marx. It demonstrates if you grasp the concepts or not, but usually doesn't do much more than that on its own.

Sometimes you can make an interesting point with those analogies, but only if you can use that association to point at the allegorical configuration of two or more other ideas. (Our inferences about a Qabbalistic framework in *Final Fantasy VII* is to X as Y is to Z.)

So, for example, we're not actually pointing to a deeper relationship which could be represented through the example of the relationship of characters in this game, if we so choose. But we the point of the analysis is in the deep structure, not in scrutinizing the game itself. It's just a tool being used to paint a picture, so we can glimpse an *underlying* pattern or relationship.

This kind of analysis is alright. We've done some of it on Modern Mythology.net, for instance, looking at various vampire or apocalypse myths in the media. But this is generally done to get a glimpse at a larger process at work.

We want to look at those deeper trends, the holographic or fractal view one can catch by blowing things up or scaling them down, twisting them around, looking at them in a way that most people might not consider. That has been the process throughout this book, and if you're still with us, chances are you are well acquainted. We can only do this through an allegory or metaphor, even in an essay.

That is what I would hope to do whether we're talking about *Buffy the Vampire Slayer*, the "end of history," or both. This approach to analysis is not about 1:1, synchronic analogies, such as "what Hindu goddesses correspond to the character in Buffy?" instead it provides a new vantage point– top down, bottom up, laterally, or perhaps we toss the entire board into chaos and imply no spatial orientation between the metaphors being employed whatsoever.

So we're looking at games and myth, right, that's what we're here to do– but we want to cut deeper than just sifting through video games and finding the shallow points of overlap between myth and gaming, like when a mythological character appears, or even when the plot-line of a game follows a pattern in a myth– unless if we can draw something insightful out of that association.

To our topic.

In biology, there's the argument that *competition* drives evolution, and there is a counter-argument that there are *co-operative* factors.

We've already taken a look at these two myths. We've talked about competition and cooperation as ways that we can view evolutionary progress. Where do we find that in gaming? Do some games emphasize one rather than the other, and what are the results of that emphasis? In a narrative sense? In terms of the gamer or participant? The game system elements of competition and cooperation can apply to anything, even SEO. Our world really is a sprawling hub of networked information, and the deep structures of hierarchies are myth-dependent.

A lot of the material written about gaming and its social or cultural effects are some kind of alarmist noise, or they come out in support of gaming. Books and articles are constantly re-acting to this. The first time I can recall it being a mainstream myth I was aware of was around the time of the Tipper Gore family values thing, and the ripples off of that. I'm sure it began before then. (Somewhere near the dawn of civilization, if it is the alarmism sprung from parents not understanding their adolescents.)

All such stories have stats peppered throughout to prove their point, and they all allow an opportunity to take a position and spin it towards an overarching thesis. Internet, rock music, porn are all destroying our brains. "Video games are destroying our attention span," is another popular myth of this camp, but I wonder what more useful myths that could be read into these cultural occurrences.

What about a myth such as "games are a fundamental part of how we learn about ourselves and the world around us, and game design that realizes this also must take responsibility for that role, and thus far it does not"? Is that question too hard to formulate, so we just go for the cheap fear reaction to sell magazines? Can't go wrong with fear, right? *Your children are being brainwashed by evil technology!*

But if we do ask that question, suddenly knowledge of the mythic implications of gaming becomes of utmost importance. The only way to know the cultural effects of a myth are to understand the interplay of narratives and results in a cultural setting. Our axiomatic moral myths will sculpt any kind of moral *conclusions* that we'd draw from this kind of analysis. Throw these out as garbage. We should consider competition and cooperation independent of the ability to sow a fear myth out of that analysis.

However, it would seem that competition is the *only* model being employed up until very recently in the gaming world– as the power of cooperation is finally getting its due in conventions and TED talks, if not as much in mainstream gaming with some notable exceptions. In *The Immanence of Myth*, Stephen Hershey gave us a brief exploration of the military and the utilization of war myths in video games to recruit and train, and how these games and the overarching military rhetoric forms a myth that draws in their would-be converts. But that just means they understand something about how to market. Why can't we also sell intelligence, creativity, collaboration? Why can't we sell education and team-work without making it hokey and awful? The moral failure isn't the military using these things. *It's that no one else does.* The fact the military knows games are great recruitment and training tools and yet the schooling system does not? Unconscionable.

What role do games play in our lives and development? Animals play to learn or at least hone almost all their skills. Wolves, chimps, killer whales, wolverines, they all learn to hunt through play, and learn most social games through games as well which factor into their very survival (and thus *evolution*) in the long run. The same is true for us. Much of what we don't think of as game *is*, especially in the social sphere, and again the role of competitive vs. cooperative games is key. We learn by play. Somewhere along the way we forgot this, perhaps by the needs of industry, which don't so much care about our *learning* so much as our *productivity*.

Another layer of game analysis is "what is a game?" and the best place to begin to answer that question is Wittgenstein's language games.

> *The rules of language (grammar) are analogous to the rules of games; meaning something in language is thus analogous to making a move in a game. The analogy between a language and a game brings out the fact that only in the various and multiform activities of human life do words have meaning. (The concept is not meant to suggest that there is anything trivial about language, or that language is 'just a game', quite the contrary.)*

We can also call to mind Wittgenstein's idea of family resemblance. Games may be many things, which do not bear direct relations to each other. They may mean different things, as well, to different participants. When you play hide and go seek with a child, it is different than when children play it with one another. Our reasons for playing them differ, and they in many ways encompass the whole of our social activity, which yet again is not to reduce it and say "it is all just a game," but rather to say that the idea of game theory applies to all group activities. It also means– and this is something I have been trying to convince corporations of for years to no avail– that learning and productivity can oftentimes be made fun without resorting to cheesy bullshit like "casual Friday."

We can bring work and play together as part of the ongoing experience of our lives as social beings, and if you don't think what I just said logically follows from that Wittgenstein quote, then you obviously don't roll with seven gram rocks. This is a part of any adaptive management philosophy, which I will proudly say in a sentence right next to another that ended with "seven gram rocks," because being passionate about our work and our play is how *we* roll, and anyone who says that can never happen is already dead, they just don't know it yet.

To get back to the quotation that started this article, you can also find a new perspective on the idea of "game" in Alternate Reality Games (ARGs), and Dave Szulborski's book *This Is Not A Game* is one of the best introductions to this subject from this very question, "what is a game?" through modern examples of game both as marketing device and art form. Tasks that might be seen as overwhelming, tedious, or even horrible can be turned into crowdsourced games that leverage the mind of the crowd towards finding satisfying answers, so long as the myths of the game support that final result.

> *I cannot stress enough that planning a framework for true and open collaboration may seem like a contradiction in terms, but it clearly is not. Some preliminary planning and construction of a workflow environment is integral to having a productive collaborative experience. Don't be afraid to plan but also keep in mind that as you progress and learn you will need to adjust and adapt. Building a framework allows for both while also providing a working space from which to launch a killer user experience. When faced with a challenge or dilemma, just remember: "Something's staring you straight in the face."* **This Is Not A Game, Foreword by Joseph Matheny, Szulborski**

ARGs are a good means of looking at social interaction as a form of marketing, and how this platform can be leveraged to explore a multi-dimensional narrative, or sell a product or idea. Crowdsourcing of activities can also be used for research, as we see in the arrival of Massively Multiplayer Online Research Environments (MMORE). Certainly, the possibilities are only limited by what we can creatively encode into the system of a game. If game designers make a certain behavior entertaining for the public, it is likely a great deal of work and group thought can be "outsourced" in this way.

However, there is a lot of tension that exists between the way that "The Suits" see these games working, and the way that creatives would like to utilize them to tell a narrative. These goals are not mutually exclusive. Profit can be means or motive. Some rather bizarre and ethically dubious ends could be drawn from these means. You could create an ARG with transmedia elements that, for instance, spun Google's attention away from a news story. (More accurately, one would for instance, crowdsource thousands of false positives, driving a semantic wedge between two items that an organization might want dissociated.)

Yes, I'm talking about crowdsourcing SEO espionage through the use of narratives that get pushed to a large enough audience. You can be sure people are already doing it. (But no, we're not going to do it for you unless you pay us a lot of money.)

Perhaps thankfully, many companies don't see these possibilities. Despite recognition of the positive ways that narrative and business can be married through long term partnerships, so much business-think has been consumed by short-term profit and shareholder terror that it can be difficult to actually bring a creative enterprise near bean-counters without sterilizing the whole operation.

Nevertheless, this is a way that business and art, mythos and logos, could be re-married. Some corporations have thought about ARGs as a simple adjunct to traditional marketing, rather than understanding that the engagement of the audience can involve their brand and products without being *solely* about their brand and products.

For example, Audi wants to help give their traditional marketing campaign a little push so they organize a game called "Art of the Heist" that popularizes the A3 before it is released, creating a mystique around this yet-to-be-released model. Products can be placed in the social sphere through actors and other plants. These can be tied into a transmedia campaign as well.

But the thing that "Suits" don't seem to understand about these games is that any long-term success is attained through the narratives or myths *themselves*. In other words, there can be a dollars and cents benefit to a good story in the so-called "long tail." What defines a "good" story, in terms of the engagement of a specific audience? This is part of the problem. It can't, or I daresay, shouldn't be quantified.

Business is the art of risk-taking. Pony up.

Similarly, education can be entertaining and collaborative, rather than tedious and competitive. A lot of people are running scared right now, and that's having an effect on what gets funded, but I think we all know that to keep *competitive*, (or was it collaborative?) Content that engages is only a start.

I believe that what we're all really looking for is the thing that's going to *transform* us.

We are always teaching one another with the games we play, even when we don't realize we're playing games. And many myths about fun and play, and seriousness and productivity, are a hindrance to not only our actual productivity but also our health. The myth that learning is not fun, that intelligence is not sexy, that education must be performed in an industrialized, factory-model approach that emphasize competition and rote memorization, is demonstrably detrimental in every way except perhaps for "units per minute." This mechanization absolutely obliterates the sacred in each and every one of us, however, and this is not a trade worth making. If we think of humans as anything other than robots, then we need to completely revolutionize how we look at games and gaming, work and working. We need to re-interpret productivity and what is truly valuable. And all of that could be done, ironically enough, when we pick up a controller.

So, to conclude: if games are a natural way that we learn and interact, if they can be used to disseminate memes and behavior patterns, then why are we consistently funding and providing energy to only certain types of games? That is the first question that this article has sought to articulate.

A revolution of how we conceive of games, and of gaming in general, could transform how we work and play, it could even transform our relationship with one another. But as always the question remains: where will this begin, and why does it remain so much easier to virtualize greed and hostility than compassion and cooperation? More importantly, how do we overcome this issue without wasting our time with empty, psuedo-moralistic hand-wringing?

Clearly, to be explored thoroughly this idea could easily fill a book and quite a few classes. So I am raising these issues for consideration toward that end, likely in someone else's hands. (And it'd be ludicrous to assume that some people aren't already, in a vaguely similar way.)

Conversation with

Raymond Salvatore Harmon

Born in the middle of nowhere Raymond Salvatore Harmon has wandered the earth, building things out of nothing, constructing realities from vague indifference and cultivating a prolonged distaste for both academia and any kind of manual labor.

RSH: *"At all levels, ultimately graffiti is an act of cultural insurgency. It is a rebellion; against the norm, against society at large, against corporations, against the city or 'government.' Graffiti is the act of changing the visual environment in the public space. It doesn't matter if its a quickly scrawled tag or a well developed painting, it shouldn't be there and it is."*

James Curcio: To begin with, I'd like to hear what you think the function of graffiti art is. Maybe it has a purpose, maybe it doesn't, but even if you don't intend a purpose, a social action like that has a reaction, it serves a function. They don't necessarily all need to have the same function but I imagine when you really cut down to it there is a fairly small range of possibilities there. What do you think?

Raymond Salvatore Harmon: Modern urban visual environments are controlled by corporations and city governments (which are in fact almost always corporations themselves). They decide where a road goes, how big signs can be, when a billboard can go up, etc. This is all dictated by financial gain. Advertising revenue plays a huge part in city planning.

When someone alters this visual landscape without permission they are fucking with the economic value of that environment. In doing so they are counteracting the attempt that the city government makes to control that environment. While the content and message can vary greatly within graffiti, the act is very clear. Graffiti is doing this act in violation of the law.

Increasingly we are seeing the growth of something that appears to be "graffiti", in that it has co-opted graffiti's common visual aesthetics and techniques, but it is done with permission. "Street art" is graffiti without the teeth. When it's being done with permission it's just the same as the advertising billboards. It's part of the plan, and in being so it's devoid of the same level of depth found in an act of true vandalism.

JC: There is a certain "pay to play" element to what is considered a legal display of imagery and what is illegal. And of course, images are a form of communication. Only some ideas get broadcast, and those ideas have money behind them. Pay $10,000 for a billboard, it's legal. This reminds me a little of the "illegal" guerrilla gardens springing up in the US, where groups are taking unused plots of lands in areas where people have little option but processed awful pseudo-foods, and growing food and using it and giving away the excess for free, in accordance with the basic "rules" of permaculture. And a lot of these operations are being shut down. There's such a point of absurdity here, and none of the arguments leveled against these groups hold much water.

However, and this is a big however, the benefit of healthy food is quite obvious. The benefit provided by some art should also be just as obvious to most people, although it often is not. But much tagging and what I guess I'd have to call crappy graffiti doesn't fall into the same boat. It's not all social activism. I mean, I don't think it is. What do you think? Is there a line to be drawn here?

RSH: The food analogy is good because it underlines the basic situation with both of these concepts, that doing something that avoids the typical capitalist infrastructure is frowned upon by the capitalist government and the corporations that own it.

The quality of a piece of art doesn't make it "not art." Any form of creative expression is ultimately art. So a "crappy tag" is just as valid an expression as a well painted piece. The irony is that you are seeing cities all over the world start to protect pieces that are by famous artists that have "financial value" all the while still harassing anyone who does graffiti that isn't famous. Its not about the quality, its about the financial value.

In a society where corporations control the visual environment of the public urban space the only form of expression that makes change is one in which we attack that control variable. Are some taggers/painters/writers better than others? Sure. But does it matter who is better or worse? Not really.

JC: Hm. I think there's something interesting going on here. I agree that there is no way to arbitrate what constitutes good art or bad art. Whenever someone creates rules, someone goes and breaks them and in so doing, blows the doors open on our concepts of the nature of art. And eventually that radical approach becomes part of the establishment, and represents a new building that must be destroyed, or painted over. Banksy for instance, now his work is entering a Warhol-esque dimension of fame whereas originally it had been just illegal.

But there are two things I'd like to highlight, and I'd be interested in hearing your take on it.

First, though there's no way of arbitrating this, I think there *is* "good" art and "bad" art. Just not universally. We won't agree on what it is, and that's exactly the point, I think. By exposing our own aesthetics, we can find the Others that see the world in a vaguely similar way- or we can encounter people that shatter our way of seeing the world, and we can see it a new way. So I think it does matter that some are better than others, but probably not in the way a lot of people would think it does.

And second– as you said, graffiti is not the same as a mural. The difference is not so much that you're getting paid, rather it is what *that* represents. I believe what you're saying is that it is inherent to the nature of graffiti art that it be illegal. It seems to me that aside from defying the "pay to play" nature of the commons that corporations and politicians assume, it is inherently transgressive. I mean, the moment it becomes condoned across the board it becomes something else. It can hang in the gallery alongside Duchamp's *Fountain*.

I think there is also a line between transgression and vandalism, which is one of the reasons I think it matters if a graffiti artist is coming at it with an awareness of these things, or they're just tagging because they think it's cool.

What is the point in transgressing in that way?

RSH: Duchamp is a great example of someone whose work was transgressive and attempting to exist outside of the context of the art world but who was appropriated immediately by the art world he was trying to resist. Banksy is just the latest version of that same thing, Banksy's greatest creation is Banksy the artist, and now Banksy the brand.

The concepts of good and bad are directly related to personal experience, they have no validity outside of how an individual may experience the art. You may look at a well painted mural and think "Wow that's amazing!" and someone else is going to say "Meh, its looks like a Nike ad" and then again they may look at a sloppy tag smeared on the front of a retail shop and say "Now that's brilliant!" but to you its just a clumsy splash of paint with no context. What matters is not "good or bad" but reaction or no reaction. If you have a reaction to it then its doing its job. If you don't notice it then its not.

The fact is that real graffiti will never be condoned. That's what is so good about it. The visual aesthetics may be appropriated by the marketing world, millions of prints and t-shirts may be sold, but in no way will spraying paint over someone's building without permission be made legal.

JC: You're probably right about that. But that still doesn't answer the question- what is the point in doing it? Is there one, or does there need to be one? Of course I imagine each artist is likely to answer that in a different way- but I'm curious to know your answer.

RSH: Are you asking "What is the point of graffiti?" which I see much the same way I would see the question "What is the point of painting?" and I would give much the same answer to both questions - compulsion. You do it because you don't have any choice but to do it. Between the variables of who you are and how your environment affects you there is an internal drive that compels an artist to create, to express, and graffiti - even the seemingly talentless/pure vandalism type - is no different. Each person may have their own "reasons" for doing it, but in the end its all about not being able to not do it. Its an act of self expression, no different than playing a guitar or painting a painting.

What separates it from these other kinds of creative expression is the aggressive form that it takes. Its not being done quietly at home where no one can see or hear it. Its happening out in the world regardless of if people like it, which gives it an incredible ability, the power to communicate to the public without any intermediary involved.

JC: I think it's interesting that you came to the same general conclusion on this that I have. When I was a little younger I had a lot more I guess you could say idealism about the intention behind my work, but when you reach a certain point– when you've gone well past the bounds of practicality or even sanity to pursue your work– you have to recognize that at bottom it's a compulsion. Habits can be good or bad of course. Yoga is an example of a method of trying to reprogram physical habits of alignment and breathing. It's not all like putting a needle in your arm. But a lot of art might be a bit more like the needle than yoga. It's hard to say.

That said, there can still be an intention behind it. So I was just rooting around there for yours.

What projects are you working on now? Are you looking to go somewhere with it or is it really "chasing the dragon"?

RSH: In my life there have been two currents that have run in parallel for a long time that have just started to converge (unfortunately). On the one had I am an unrealist as an artist. Aesthetics doesn't need to have an explicit message in a semantic sense. Language often simplifies something that can be more complex than any set of verbal descriptions. Burroughs said that language is a virus and I would have to agree with that.

So creatively, as a painter, I have sought out form and colour as a way of expressing myself without the need for some kind of philosophic message. I see all art as simply experience and nothing more. First there is the experience of the artist in creating the work. The process, the interaction with the medium as a form of expression, the dance. Secondly art is the experience of perceiving it. Of looking at at, hearing it, touching, even tasting in the moment of the audience/viewers perceptual awareness. Besides this two sided coin of experience there is nothing.

Alongside of this current of creative expression has always been a very distinct outlook on the world's socio-political stage. Call it an interest in contemporary urban anthropology (which is my education background) I have always had strong opinions on what I call the "disconnect" that most people live in, a kind of strangely exclusive filter bubble that lets people get on with living without acknowledging that totally corrupt and insanely designed socio-cultural box we are told we have to live in. It started in my teens, I was really into social anarchism and the writings of Giovanni Baldelli at age 15, around the time the Tienanmen Square events occurred and it shaped my outlook on the media and the governments of the world.

So now I find these two currents spilling over into each other despite many years of keeping them separate. But in general I see all of my interests starting to converge as we move into the future. The media work, the painting, the writing (which is my least favorite thing to do) are all coming together. There may be another book at some point, but really I guess I am just chasing the dragon.

Conversation with

Aunia Kahn about the Silver Era Tarot

Aunia Kahn's *work combines many disciplines, wrapping them into a hybrid art form melding photography, painting and collage. She invariably designs, builds, and executes characters, non-existent places, dreams, illusions, fears and fables into creation, which meld elements of classical, and contemporary art. Each work makes use of her own likeness in movie-like stills, dealing in varied taboo and often controversial subject matter to challenge the viewer, their understanding and preconceived notions; yet she connects through honest feeling and emotions. Aunia's work has constantly evolved, earlier works dealt more with her past, while her more recent creations delve into present emotional conflicts and inspirations.*

James Curcio: I tend to look at Tarot more as a collection of archetypes, an arrangement that can be used to create some pretty primal narratives. I'm curious to know what your perspective on it is. How did you put together the symbolism for the deck?

Aunia Kahn: The deck was based on the original symbolism of the Ryder Waite deck. The symbolism from such an influential deck in the tarot community is something that you either embrace or stray away from. If you stay away from traditional symbolism with your deck, it can be considered a non-usable "art deck", rather than a fully functioning deck.

It's like Monopoly. If you create boards with different themes or designs, but stick to the traditional ideas of the game and how it's played– then it works, yet if you changed everything and made it your own thing, it would become a new game all together. The symbolism of the Ryder Waite was the basis of where we started the foundation of our works and then I created artwork telling the same tale but in my own style and followed the journey of the deck while doing so.

JC: It's true that if the symbolism you use isn't accessible to people, it'll fail as a Tarot deck if not a work of art. However, there are many arrangements other than Ryder Waite. The symbolism of Crowley's Thoth deck was always the most accessible to me, which is somewhat surprising considering how obscure and esoteric some of the philosophy behind it is. Of course, without the accompanying book, it would've been even more opaque to most audiences. Was part of the intent in creating a companion book for this project to help people grasp variations in symbolism? Or is it a more general guide to Tarot?

AK: Although the deck does have its own symbolism, the creation of the companion book itself was meant, as you said, to be more of a general introduction with some of our own interpretations. We saw the Silver Era Tarot as a project that could, and has, brought new users into the realm of exploration. We only desired to give a very small tickler of information to inspire others to research or discover for themselves what tarot could mean in their own lives; there is so much information available, it wouldn't have been possible to write something so encompassing.

JC: How much was from Russell and how did that collaboration work?

AK: Originally I was going to create both the art and write the book for the deck, but found working collaboratively with a very good writer would help my idea be more solid and I could focus solely on the art.

As a collaborative project, Russell came in as the writer of the companion book, and I got to focus on just the artwork and layout. We worked alone on both of our specialties, but always ran the final products of each section by each other. I created the cards in order of where I was on my journey, so it was all feeling with no specific order. Russell on the other hand wrote the book from front to back, Major Arcana through the Minors in order in which they would appear. When the book and deck was finalized, we both took turns looking over the finalized art and writing to make sure that we had found a delicate balance with both of our works.

JC: Was there a lot of research involved, or was it a personal process?

AK: For myself there was a ton of research that began with each card I worked on. I wanted to make sure I saw all the different takes on the cards, and was able to find my own emotions and understanding of each card before I created the art. Then setting up each artwork in lines with the original symbolism but making sure that I created something original and fluent was challenging but a great journey. Russell also had a lot of research to do as well, we shared a lot of what we found together and came to a middle ground.

JC: How does personal as well as traditional mythology influence your work...or does it?

AK: Overall this was a informative and fun journey for both of us, and for me a very important one. I found that each artwork was something I could use to relate to my personal mythology and find answers, clues and even ways to change my life in the present. Each card has so much to offer when you look past the surface, when doing in-depth research.

As for traditional mythology, I find that doing all the research had a direct impact on how I saw other things linking us to our past in tradition and how many of them are still present today in many cultures. I also came to understand that so many things that are found taboo are really just something we are not opening ourselves up to due to the way they are presented to us. If we started as a culture to do research rather than to take what others say as our truths we would find that we open up ourselves to something very special.

JC: I've felt for a long time that all of our suppositions...all our beliefs, even...about the world are myths, and they have yet more myths hiding underneath them. I suppose we could classify different kinds of myths, like the sort that is an involved narrative that you might find in a movie is different than the myth that there is a subconscious, or the myth that some people hold matter to be "real," or mind to be "real"... But it essentially boils down to the same thing. So I certainly agree that delving into and questioning our beliefs can open up new possibilities, although that's not to say that I think there is any conclusion to that process. Socrates' "I know one thing, that I know nothing," is the closest we've got to wisdom.

What first interested you in tarot? And if I can go beyond the scope of this particular project, when did you first consider yourself an artist? Did that shift of identity change anything, do you think?

AK: Tarot has always had a fascination in my mind, but like many people I didn't experience it until it was the right time, that time came as early as 2005 as I made the plunge (although inadvertently at first) to being an artist. When you hear about people 'always knowing' they were meant to be something specific it is amazing to hear, but with me it wasn't that way, yes, I was creative in many ways for as long as I can remember, but my art as we know it was not originally created for public consumption, it was created as a form of self-healing from a past of turmoil. Only when I was prompted to exhibit my works did I even give thought to that possibility. As I have embraced and furthered myself, the identity of course changes; a person grows and becomes what they believe they want to be.

There are no shortages of struggles, doubts and tests that make one question their path, and if there is anything we all learn throughout life, change is inevitable. My works, motivations and abilities have changed to reflect a growth and expansion in themes from the calm and peaceful to the challenging.

So in a nutshell, yes it did change many things.

JC: And in the process of externalizing that as *art*, other people can possibly find something transformative as well.

Conversation With

Charles Eisenstein about Sacred Economics

I was introduced to Charles Eisenstein through Daniel Pinchbeck, to talk about his book Sacred Economics, which is published by Evolver Editions.

As we talked, it became apparent to me that we've both worked on projects with many similar intentions, and so there seems to be an element of serendipity involved here. I offered the opportunity to post here on Modern Mythology, so you will likely be hearing more from him in the future.

I hope you enjoy the conversation we had about myth, post-economics, and the apocalyptic, evolutionary challenges facing us all.

James Curcio: It seems to me that you're taking a lot of the issues now facing us as a species– economically and environmentally– and posing them as challenges.

It has long seemed to me that there is a sort of "evolve or die" challenge posed to us as a direct result of our own actions, and it's best to face those challenges with optimism rather than pessimism. Much of that challenge arises from the myth of the individual and our unwillingness to bring that back to actions for the greater collective good. It can be hard to remain optimistic in light of that.

Charles Eisenstein: It isn't so much that I see the crises we face as challenges, but as the drivers of a transformational process. I guess you could call them challenges– but only in the sense that they challenge the basic mythology of our civilization. They are not bumps in the road that we can overcome and continue our trajectory. As you mention, one of the primary, defining myths of our civilization is the "myth of the individual," or what I would call our "story of self"– that we are discrete, separate beings living in an objective universe, bubbles of psychology isolated in genetically-determined flesh robots, seeking to maximize self-interest. I think that the crises converging upon us are making this story of self untenable, as we become most painfully aware that what we do unto the other, we do unto ourselves.

JC: I'm very familiar with this idea. It seems we've developed a similar lexicon, which is unsurprising if this really is a movement on a scale where it could possibly have any effect. It has to be bigger than all of us.

CE: I think it is only helpful to face our challenges with optimism if that optimism is authentic. If it is fake optimism, a veneer of positive thinking over a black hole of despair (I've certainly been there!) then on some level we know we are fooling ourselves, and we cannot act effectively or speak persuasively.

169

I am indeed optimistic, but it is an optimism fully cognizant of the magnitude of the crisis. Things are worse than almost anyone thinks, even the doomsayers. I am optimistic, though, because of how transformation happens, whether on an individual or collective level. It is something like this:

The old world falls apart and, after a time in the chaotic void-space between worlds, a new world is born. Or we are born into it. So I think the crises of our time are a kind of birthing— they are the birth pangs of mother earth. It is painful, and even dangerous, but it can't happen any other way.

JC: Yes. A good premise for mythic fiction as well as a very possible future.

I also think the conditions we face serve as a stress test, where, as you say, entire paradigms need to be reborn. A lot of times the amount of work that such an endeavor demands can only happen after a tragedy. There's a tragedy in Japan with a nuclear reactor and suddenly people begin questioning the efficacy of what's been in our backyards for decades. And I don't say this to imply that hysteria is the modern version of Hegelian logic.

I think that systemic shifts only happen through the level of myths first, and then through the rest of society. People say ideas are empty and it's true that talk is cheap. But myths drive the world, and if those don't shift, in this regard, nothing else will.

CE: I agree with you and I'm happy to know other people understand the importance of myth, and the extent to which it creates our world even today. I usually call it "story" not myth, but we are really talking about the same thing. Sure, on one level they are just words, and people often tell me they are sick of words and more words; they want to take action. On the other hand, though, in a socially-created world, words are actions. When Obama "takes action" he does so by saying something or signing something. Congress "takes action" by writing long documents. The symbols that they wield carry power because of the stories in which they are embedded.

We can feel these stories wearing thin today though— our defining myths are losing their power. That is one reason why I think that the time is ripe to create new myths. Well, not really to "create" in the usual sense, but to tap into them, receive them, spread them, and serve them.

JC: I completely agree. It's what I've dedicated my life to. Would you say that is true for you as well?

CE: Well, yes I suppose, though it took me a long while to figure that out, to figure out why I am here. I think all of us, each in a unique way, is on earth at this time to serve the emergence of what I call The More Beautiful World our Hearts Tell us is Possible. That service could be quite public, or it could be nearly invisible— taking care of a dying person or an abandoned animal— but on some level all of us hear the call. In my case, it took a lot of years of wandering before I finally listened to it. One purpose of my work is to tell people, "Yes, I hear it too, go for it!" so that they needn't wander as long as I did. When there is no one reinforcing that heart-knowing of a more beautiful world, one suspects that maybe one is crazy. We feel alone.

JC: Yes. However, I am curious how you see this transformation occurring realistically when there are so many cultural forces in place designed specifically to stop it until it has already reached a point of no return. For instance, the corporate land-grab for land as well as water and energy resources...

CE: It is true that certain forces will do their best to keep the Machine running as long as possible, just as an alcoholic will sometimes destroy his entire life just to keep the addiction going a little longer. In fact, our relationship to technology, to debt-money, to consumption, is very much like an addiction. It is indeed possible, as you say, for our emergence into a new realm to be stillborn; sometimes the alcoholic only hits bottom on his deathbed. That is why we cannot just sit back and wait for the collapse to happen. Before it does, we must actively "raise bottom", so that when things fall apart, there will be enough natural, cultural, and spiritual wealth remaining to nourish the next phase of humanity.

JC: Of course, it's interesting to me when we start posing The Machine as a negative thing. There's a lot of myths that have been born out of machine-anxiety, whether it's *Metropolis* or we see the psychological ramifications of it crystallized in Orwell's *1984*. The biggest challenge of understanding mythology is seeing beyond the ethical binaries our own myths create.

All that said, I think we can both agree that we prefer the kind of technology represented by the Lifestraw– a device that lets you turn dirty water, even sewage, into drinkable water– than genetically owned non-heirloom seeds. And that's what this really comes down to, isn't it? Asking that our technology be as controlled by humanitarian ethics as profit?

CE: Certain environmental behaviors can be profitable, but if we are to justify and motivate them based on profit, then we are implicitly validating profit, legitimizing profit as an ally of change. That would be okay if it were, but usually it is not. My work in economics is largely devoted to changing the money system to align money with ecology at the base level. After all, money is supposed (in an ideal world) to represent the gratitude of society for an individuals contribution to the common good. Why, then, do we have a money system in which you can make money by cutting down a forest and building a housing development, but if you want to restore a forest to serve the planet and future generations, well, there's no money in that? The answer has little to do with greed, but is inherent in the way money today is created and circulates.

JC: There's still a deeper question here, just how long the gravity of the status quo will keep us locked in as a society. I see an increasing number of people blinking and looking around like, "wait a second! This is insane! We've been *had!*" But no one seems to really know what to do about it.

CE: In a way it is good that they don't know what to do about it, for now. That's because, one: so many of our conditioned responses are ineffectual or actually end up strengthening the status quo and deepening our servitude. I'm thinking of the rebellious high school student who knows he's being had and lashes out by setting off a smoke bomb in the lavatory, thereby reinforcing the myth of the necessity of controlling these bad kids, and controlling the animal nature of all of us... and he learns that resistance is futile, and learns to be ashamed of himself.... Oh, and two: we don't really have a new mythology, as you would put it, to guide our actions. But I think the time is ripe for one.

Even if people don't know what to do, they believe less and less in the status quo, and therefore participate in it less and less fully. Their partial withdrawal accelerates its demise. In an earlier era, I would not be doing what I am today. I'd probably be cheerfully participating in the program of dominating nature. But by the time I came of age, that story, that myth that I call "Ascent," was no longer compelling.

http://partyattheworldsend.com/

Fallen Nation: Party At The World's End
is a mad ride past the event horizon of sanity with
a group of young, escaped mental patients that come
to realize—or believe—that they are demigods.
They form Babylon, a band that captures the spirit
of the age as sex, drugs, and chaos reign in the
final years of the American Empire.

This is the beginning of a modern mythology that
spills off the page: the ticket to the Party At The
World's End is inside, if you dare to search for it.
It starts right here, but it won't end here——